Miriam Halfmann

'The bastards are
making it up!'

Miriam Halfmann

'The bastards are making it up!' –
Forms of New Journalism in Norman Mailer's *The Armies of the Night* and Truman Capote's *In Cold Blood*

Tectum Verlag

Miriam Halfmann

'The bastards are making it up!' –
Forms of New Journalism in
Norman Mailer's *The Armies of the Night*
and Truman Capote's *In Cold Blood*

ISBN: 978-3-8288-2424-9
Umschlagabbildung: © peepo | istockphoto.com
© Tectum Verlag Marburg, 2010

Besuchen Sie uns im Internet
www.tectum-verlag.de

Bibliografische Informationen der Deutschen Nationalbibliothek
Die Deutsche Nationalbibliothek verzeichnet diese Publikation in der
Deutschen Nationalbibliografie; detaillierte bibliografische Angaben sind
im Internet über http://dnb.ddb.de abrufbar.

Table of Contents

1 The Clash of Genres – Introduction 9

2 A Short History of 'Faction' – Backgrounds to and Developments of New Journalism 15

2.1 "These Have Been the Years of Conformity and Depression" – Moments of the American 1950s and 1960s 15

2.2 From Eisenhower to Johnson – Between 'Wealth' and Depression 16

2.3 Rebelling or 'Dropping Out'? – The Counter Culture of the 1950s and 1960s 21

    2.3.1 'Anything Goes' – Mass Culture and Postmodernism 26

2.4 Making up the News – The Coming of 'Faction' 32

    2.4.1 What's the News? – Incidents and Ideals in 19th- and 20th-Century American Journalism 33

    2.4.2 The New Journalism and the Nonfiction Novel – What are we talking about? 38

3 Self-Reflexivity as a Path to Personal Truth – Norman Mailer's *The Armies of the Night: History as a Novel, the Novel as History* 47

3.1 "Let us then make our comic hero the narrative vehicle' – Self-Reflexivity, Metafiction, and Mailer's Very Own 'Return of the Author' 49

3.2 "Like most cloudy metaphors, this served to get him home" – Style and Figurative Language 59

3.3 "History as a Novel, the Novel as History" – The Interrelation between Form and Contents 66

4	A (Re-)Construction of Truth – Truman Capote's *In Cold Blood: A True Account of a Multiple Murder and Its Consequences* 73
4.1	Gazing, Commenting, Silencing – The Narrative Technique 75
4.2	The Facts Do No Longer Speak For Themselves – Style and Figurative Language 85
4.3	The Novel as Prison – Form as Meaning 91
5	**Conclusion** **97**
6	**Bibliography** **103**

»Literature is the art of writing something
that will be read twice;
journalism what will be grasped at once.«
(Connolly 19)

1 The Clash of Genres – Introduction

When English writer and literary critic Cyril Connolly implies that literary texts must be read several times in order to be fully comprehended, whereas journalistic texts virtually 'open up' to people, he describes a common notion: Literature is generally felt to be rather complex; journalism is thought of as straightforward and associated with a rather plain, unadorned style.

While the different functions of literature and journalism make it hard to see why one should be preferred to the other, a hierarchy between literature and journalism did indeed develop by and by. In the U.S., as Michael Schudson, sociologist and historian of American journalism, points out, especially in its early forms at the beginning of the 19th century, journalism was often said to be "'corrupting,' 'vulgar,' and without decency" (Schudson a, 13). By quoting from novelist James Fenimore Cooper's *The American Democrat* (1838), Schudson illustrates the perception of journalism at that time as "tyranniz[ing] over publick men, letters, the arts, the stage, and even private life" by acting "under the pretence of protecting publick morals" (Cooper qtd. in ibid.). And even today, journalism and literature are more often than not conceived of as "two separate spheres (one 'low', the other 'high')" (Keeble/Wheeler 2), in which "the journalist is considered an inferior species compared, say, to the writer of novels or history" (Ingrams qtd. in ibid.).

However, if the focus shifts to people who create literary texts, numerous cases of journalistic moonlighting are known. Richard Keeble, professor of journalism, points to the fact that the widespread association between journalism and mass culture[1] caused authors to justify their journalistic 'excursions' (ibid. 4). As in the case of William Hazlitt, many of them used to speak of a "'higher' journalism" they claimed to be practicing (ibid.). But even though this hierarchical dichotomy did to some extent last until today, a basal common ground between literature and journalism can be established.

Among the respective 'sub-genres' of literature and journalism, striking similarities can be detected. It is, for example, interesting to see that the insertion of the term story in the journalistic term 'news story' implies a certain focus on "the *aesthetic* object of a narrative" (Chatman 27, my italics) and, thus, triggers a direct association with literature and the art of storytelling. And indeed, as Schudson explains, the news story

---

[1] People associated journalism with mass culture since the term 'journalist,' which was imported from France, referred to a writer of periodicals as opposed to a writer of literature (Keeble/Wheeler 4).

is, like the feature (story), openly requested to not only report but also to "offer a kind of commentary on public life" (Schudson b, 179). Belonging to the category of 'soft news,' the news story is thus opposing 'hard news' which "focus[] on who, what, where, when, why [...] containing little description, journalist comment or analysis" (Keeble 304). Doubtlessly, certain forms of journalism are very close to literature, and such similarities are even being loosely explored by the academy. But as to where do journalism and literature strikingly differ? For a start, the two concepts seem to diverge considerably when it comes to their respective references. Literature is traditionally said to refer to an imaginary reality; journalism is meant to focus on a socially binding reality (Blöbaum/ Neuhaus 34). Like the following example, probably every other definition of the term 'journalism' will prove that its reference to contemporary reality is commonly agreed on:

> Journalism is the business or practice of producing and disseminating information about *contemporary* affairs of general public interest and importance. It is the business of a set of institutions that publicizes periodically (usually daily) information and commentary on *contemporary* affairs, normally presented as true and sincere, to a dispersed and anonymous audience so as to publicly include the audience in a discourse taken to be publicly important. (Schudson b, 11, my italics)

So far, this difference between literature and journalism has never been explicitly contested. But what happens if suddenly whole books appear which are concerned with contemporary, everyday issues, make a truth claim, and, on top of that, read more like literature than the best feature story? What does it mean when genres clash and boundaries start to blur?

Referring to the U.S. mid-1960s, journalist Tom Wolfe sensed a certain "artistic excitement in journalism" (Wolfe 37), which was for him "a new thing in itself," (ibid.) and rapidly evolved into what Wolfe was to name "new journalism." As this revolutionary trend in American journalism – and, as it was to turn out, also American letters in general – will constitute the overall subject matter of this study, an introductory sketch of its emergence can best be provided by referring to Wolfe's preface of his study and anthology *The new journalism*, first published in 1973. When in 1965, as a response to his article entitled "Tiny Mummies! The True Story of the Ruler of 43rd Street's Land of the Walking Dead!", the Columbia Journalism Review and The New York Review of Books accused Wolfe of having written a piece of 'parajournalism,' he showed himself surprised. In his opinion, he had simply penned an "'essay' of the old school" (ibid. 38). At about the same time, his colleagues Jimmy

Breslin and Gay Talese had to cope with similar finger pointing. Rather amused with such excitement, Wolfe did not really care about the hostility. However, he was well aware that his article must have (accidentally) worked against an unsaid but commonly known hierarchy within a system regarding journalists as the "lower class" and novelists as "the literary upper class" (ibid. 39). He must have unconsciously tried to shoot to fame by writing like a novelist. Curiously, by and by, he himself witnessed how feature writers increasingly considered "that it just might be possible to write journalism that would [...] read like a novel" (ibid. 21). Soon, Wolfe decided to 'go with the flow,' feeling that "it was time someone violated what Orwell had called 'the Geneva conventions of the mind'," meaning "a protocol that had kept journalism and non-fiction generally (and novels) in such a tedious bind for so long" (ibid. 36). For him, the new-found "esthetic dimension" of journalism became manifest in "the discovery that it was possible in non-fiction, in journalism, to use any literary device [...] and to use many different kinds simultaneously [...] to excite the reader both intellectually and emotionally" (ibid. 28). Stylistically, he characterized the fictionalizing techniques of new journalism as simply "more spectacular" (ibid. 62) than everything else on the journalistic (and the literary) scene.

Significantly, at the same time, more and more U.S. novelists were refraining from taking up contemporary issues as subjects of their works. Instead of dealing with what Wolfe regarded as "the richest terrain of the novel: society, the social tableau, manners and morals" (ibid. 43), writers like Thomas Pynchon or John Barthes responded to an increasingly violent reality, characterized by political assassinations and futile wars, by revisiting forms of fable and myth. This seemed like the perfect chance for the new journalists to pitch in. Turning the tables, now Wolfe was the one to cheer since "[t]he – New Journalists – Parajournalists – had the whole crazed obscene uproarious Mammon-faced drug-soaked mau-mau lust-oozing Sixties in America all to themselves" (ibid. 45). It is hardly surprising that the new journalists soon lost all respect for what Wolfe had once described as "the reigning literary artist" (ibid. 22), the novelist. In his very own, quite boastful tone, Wolfe declared: "If a new literary style could originate in journalism, then it stood to reason that journalism could aspire to more than mere emulation of those aging giants, the novelists." (ibid. 36) And to provoke the novelists even more, he added that "[t]he crucial part that reporting plays in all story-telling [...] [wa]s something that [wa]s not so much ignored as simply not comprehended" (ibid. 27) so that "[i]t took the New Journalism to bring this strange matter of reporting into the foreground" (ibid. 28).

While the new journalists did not establish a school (Hollowell 15), they still had a powerful impact on the literary landscape of the sixties.

In *The Kandy-Kolored Tangerine-Flake Streamline Baby* (1965), a collection of Wolfe's essays, he wrote on personalities nobody had been interested in so far, such as custom-car designers or topless dancers. Quite contrarily, in *Dispatches* (1968) Michael Herr gave an account of his experience of the war in Vietnam during his time as a correspondent for the *Esquire*. These two books are prime examples of the wide scope of new journalistic coverage, and they are united in their authors' conviction that the techniques of conventional journalism were not suitable for painting an adequate picture of the events and the persons covered.

In this book, the development and the characteristics of new journalism are to be traced more closely. Doubtlessly, journalism was at all times linked with social realities, and the new journalists' decision to refrain from conventional reporting was, among other things, highly influenced by the particularly extreme events and social upheavals of the 1960s. Therefore, the introduction will be followed by a sketch of the situation of the U.S. from the late 1950s to the 1960s, the era in which new journalism had its heyday. This socio-cultural contextualization is to start off with an overview of the economic and political developments as they were in many ways responsible for the social turmoil. Subsequently, the subversive role of the counter culture of the 1950s and 1960s as well as the significance of the underlying cultural concepts mass culture and postmodernism will be highlighted. As the new journalists gave accounts of the contemporary particularities and pressures they dealt with, this draft aims to convey in how far new journalism was informed by its time.

It is striking that there is little critical literature exclusively concerned with new journalism, and that many of these studies were published in the late 1970s or early 1980s. Thus, the concept of new journalism remains, as John C. Hartsock notes, "largely unexamined by the academy" (2). It is therefore vital to include a chapter on the coming of 'faction,' a more overall term indicating a preoccupation with facts that takes into account a fictional quality of real-life matters. As this section aims to offer a perspective for a deeper understanding of the development and the nature of new journalism, it will be divided into two parts. In the first part the changing ideals in American journalism from the 19th to the mid-20th century are to be traced briefly. In so doing, the journalistic origin of new journalistic works is acknowledged, whereas the focus will be put on the development of the subjectivity/objectivity binary. Narrowing the scope to the questions of what objective or subjective news coverage entailed, and why the one or the other was favored, is supposed to help comprehend the new journalists' tendency to refrain from the ideal of objectivity and to create increasingly personal accounts that were nevertheless committed to truth. The second part of the chapter ties in by negotiating scholarly views on the nature of new journalism and the nonfiction novel as well as on the new journalists' motivation to create their hybrid style. Considering that scholarly discussions of new journalism are comparatively rare and that views sometimes diverge, the general aim is an approximation to the new journalism and the nonfiction novel with regard to their generic features.

The socio-cultural and the theoretical framework will be supplemented by the analyses of two prominent works of new journalism. As close readings of new journalistic works are widely lacking in critical literature, these analyses constitute the slightly larger part of the study and are to provide a more practical approach to a somewhat elusive concept. The works to be examined are Norman Mailer's *The Armies of the Night: History as a Novel, the Novel as History* (1968) and Truman Capote's *In Cold Blood: A True Account of a Multiple Murder and Its Consequences* (1965). These two novels are selected due to their differences. *The Armies of the Night* is based on two articles Mailer wrote on the legendary Washington protest march against the war in Vietnam in October 1967. Since he acted as master of ceremony and one of the leaders of the march, the novel is mainly about his personal experiences. On account of its explicit concern with the political and social tensions of the 1960s, this novel will be scrutinized first. Among other things, *In Cold Blood* differs from Mailer's account in that Capote had to reconstruct large parts of the event he wrote on. He chose to cover a brutal family slaying in Kansas, of which he, unlike Mailer, gained the 'inside scoop' by means of detailed research. Moreover, Capote's novel is of particular interest since it is often regarded as giving birth to new journalism. It is, however, interesting to see that both novels have a central theme in common, as both subtitles indicate a very obvious preoccupation with strategies of representing reality. Due of these differences and the one striking similarity, it is the aim of the analyses to explore and negotiate the respective approaches to a depiction of reality. In order to arrive at a representative analytical outcome, both novels will be examined by looking into the same criteria: narrative technique, style and figurative language, and form[2]. It is important to notice that this approach excludes a consideration of journalistic categories other than the two basic doctrines of objectivity and subjectivity. In order to keep the analyses to a manageable length, and due to a special interest in the fictionalizing aspect of new journalism, the focus of the close reading to be done will be exclusively put on said categories, which are commonly associated with the criticism of fiction.

---

2   In the analyses, the term 'form' will be used synonymously with the term 'structure.'

Ultimately, a juxtaposition of the two different forms of new journalism offered by both novels will provide results that may elsewhere serve as the foundation of a typology of these and other new journalistic works. While the intention to arrive at a typology would involve the inclusion and the detailed analysis of a representative amount of works, this book can be seen as an incentive for a classification of new journalistic writing. Although a typology of new journalistic works will, like every other typology, necessarily have to cope with a certain fragmentariness in analyzing all characteristics, it would still allow a more differentiated approach to a genre that, even more than forty years after its development, still deserves study.

2 A Short History of 'Faction' – Backgrounds to and Developments of New Journalism

2.1 "These Have Been the Years of Conformity and Depression" – Moments of the American 1950s and 1960s

The new journalists began to create their hybrid style during one of the most disquieting periods in 20th-century American history. The extreme historical, social, and cultural events and experiences of the 1950s and 1960s had an enormous influence on the development of new journalism. On the one hand, unsettling political events and unparalleled scientific achievements as well as matters and personalities of everyday life became subjects of new journalistic writing. Mailer gave a startling account of one of the biggest demonstrations against the war in Vietnam in *The Armies of the Night* and explored the potential consequences of Neil Armstrong's moonwalk in *Of a Fire on the Moon* (1970), and George Plimpton and Hunter S. Thompson provided their readers with 'inside scoops' of what it means to be a professional football player and a member of the Hell's Angels in their novels *Paper Lion* (1966) and *Hell's Angels: A Strange and Terrible Saga* (1967). On the other hand, such events and cultural phenomena were of a more implicit importance. Events were oftentimes the trigger of a plurality of change processes within American culture and the arts. Thus, the new journalists came to write in the wake of postmodernism and mass culture and their 'literary coverage' of contemporary issues made them chroniclers of mid-20th-century American history.

Starting from Andreas Huyssen's assertion that underlying and often subversive currents in American culture "transformed inherited ideological notions of style, form and creativity" (190), the following sketches and deliberations serve to negotiate important moments and aspects of as well as scholarly views on the situation of the U.S. during the 1950s and 60s. The journalistic aspiration to tackle the nature of the "radically altered reality of America in an era of intense social change" (Hollowell 16), later to be discussed, which was informed by the euphoric rise and deep fall of an optimistic belief in government, put the new journalists to the test. Therefore, an overview of the changes and challenges the U.S. had to face during Eisenhower's and, primarily, Kennedy's and Johnson's presidencies is to be provided at first. This draft is then going to be enhanced by the exploration of an emerging counter culture and the significance of mass culture and postmodernism in altering America's cultural landscape. Generally speaking, the aim of this socio-cultural contextualization is to provide information about the backgrounds which influenced the new journalists' decision to strike a balance between journalistic reporting and literary fictionalizing while writing on contemporary issues.

2.2 From Eisenhower to Johnson – Between 'Wealth' and Depression

The Eisenhower Administration continued from 1953 to 1961 and thus decisively shaped the situation of America in the 1950s. During the fifties, the majority of the American population perceived the state of the nation as dazzling and wealthy. As a matter of fact, in the second half of the decade, per capita personal income and the GNP reached record heights, and work ethic decreased due to shorter work weeks and longer vacations (Heath 2). As Hugh Brogan puts it, "a steadily expanding market, a steadily improving standard of living for all [...] seemed to be the new law of nature" (589).

However, it was not long until critical voices were raised setting out to reveal the administration's neglects. In 1962, Michael Harrington's *The Other America* and Robert M. Hutchins' *The Higher Learning in America* constituted two of the most widely noticed analyses of diverse drawbacks in American society. Harrington's book alarmingly rebutted the claim maintained by Eisenhower that there were no poor people in the U.S., whereas Hutchins gave a startling account of the deficient American educational system.

But the crisis of the 1950s turned out to be more of an elusive, underlying nature. Since most Americans had been shaped by the anti-communism already proclaimed by McCarthy, there was not much approval of any kind of liberalism. On the contrary, the U.S. – wealthy on the surface – quite rapidly turned into a consumer culture and the fact that the 'American Way of Life' "was vindicated with every bottle of Coca-Cola sold" (Brogan 588) triggered its tendency towards conformism. This meant that the praised individualism, which had once formed the basis of the social value system of the U.S., was now falling into oblivion. As Wolfgang Riedel observes, ever since the 'American Way of Life' entered the post-industrial American society, individualism got lost in the anonymous crowd (32-33). Apart from rather isolated criticism such as Harrington's and Hutchins' accounts mentioned above or David Riesman's *The Lonely Crowd* (1950) and William H. Whyte's *The Organization Man* (1956), this loss of individual identity was not recognized by the larger part of the American middle class. However, Morris Dickstein argues that nowadays people's "selective cultural memory" tends to think of the 1950s as a time of "mindless optimism" (4). As more and more Americans moved up to the middle class, it seemed as if they took the good life they were entering as their "sovereign right" (ibid. 3) and did not (want to) pay attention to the co-existing drawbacks mentioned earlier. In the end, it was the voices of the art scene – writers, artists, and musicians – that turned this seething "deep discomfort at the core of American affluence and power," which went along with consumerism, conformity, and the rapid technological modernization resulting from America's hegemony in the world, into themes of their works (ibid. 16). "Anxiety, paranoia, and inner conflict" were recurrent themes in many forms of postwar art (ibid. 7) and laid bare the subliminal "subversive social energies roiling beneath the placid surface of the Truman and Eisenhower years" (ibid. 15). New technological advances such as the cinema and, more importantly, the television were soon attacked by cultural critics. Their popularity and content were both considered an expression of the critical state of the nation and a contribution to the precarious situation. *Film noir*, for example, offered an alternative concept to glamorous Hollywood cinema and gave an idea of an alienated society featuring pessimistic worldviews, dark coloring, and dubious, bitter characters. Many critics regarded it therefore as "perhaps the best known evidence of the dark side of postwar culture" of the late 1940s and the 1950s (ibid. 5). The television, for that matter, did not only constitute the domestic equivalent to the cinema but also the center of what Elaine Tyler May in her study *Homeward Bound: American Families in the Cold War Era* considers to be the "domestic equivalent to the containment policy," meaning a strong American focus on the domestic sphere, home and family life (ibid. 8-9). For critics of mass culture, the rise of the popular medium was therefore a thorn in their sides; their "bête noire" that triggered conformity by functioning as a gathering place for the family and made people privatize leisure time more than ever before by centering their lives on their homes (ibid. 7).

When Kennedy took office in 1961, he was eager for domestic reform, facing more than five million unemployed Americans. Among them, one to two million were permanently unemployed, which was chiefly due to an increasing mechanization. Recognizing the mood of the times, Kennedy set out to solve the nation's problems. As he sensed that they might be able to provide him with a broader insight into the drawbacks in American society and culture, he consulted renowned academics like Noam Chomsky, Nobel prize laureates, and artists. Creating this kind of exclusive 'think tank' helped him to successfully put his 'New Frontier' forward so that, in the end, his domestic and foreign programs proved to be fairly fruitful given the obstacles he had had to overcome. Having most of his reforming endeavors thwarted by Congress, he, for example, still managed to avoid economic recession and even achieved an annual 3.6 per cent GNP growth rate (Wynn 409). In order to pinpoint the merits of the Kennedy administration, historian and Kennedy expert Jim F. Heath directly compares 'JFK's style to that of Eisenhower. He concludes that Eisenhower's domestic policy may be characterized by a constant refusal to accept new social programs and a desire to preserve the *status quo* and maintain "passive leadership," which resulted in Eisenhower's "failure to mobilize public sentiment" and, thus, "the public's apathy" (7). In contrast, Kennedy must be considered an "activist[]" who "intended to rule energetically" (10).

However, political scientists often argue that Kennedy was too much concerned with foreign affairs like the Cuban Missile Crisis or the beginning of the Vietnam War while back home in the U.S. the unemployment rate was still alarming, prices were constantly rising, and most Americans were becoming aware of the existence of poverty among them (Wynn 409). So, when Kennedy was assassinated on 22 November 1963 in Dallas, Texas, vice president Lyndon B. Johnson found himself confronted with a nation whose hopes and dreams were shattered. After having uncovered the superficial nature of the 'glamorous' Eisenhower era, Kennedy had started to make good for his predecessor's defaults. It was now up to Johnson to confront America's domestic troubles.

With Lyndon B. Johnson a 'self-made man' struck out to fight poverty in America. The former high school teacher was elected to the House of Representatives in 1937, became a member of the Senate in 1948, Senate Democratic minority leader in 1953, and was re-elected president in 1964 with the then widest popular margin in the 20th century (ibid. 412).

Already in his first State of the Union Address, Johnson proclaimed a 'War on Poverty' in response to an alarmingly high national poverty rate. This battle cry was closely connected to his vision of a 'Great Society' – Johnson's set of domestic objectives aiming at "the fulfillment of the American dream of prosperity and equality for all" (Heath 10). As a part of his program, he lined up several measures. He passed, for example, a tax cut, hoping to cause a generally stable economic growth, and the Economic Opportunity Act, which intended to enable young high-school-dropouts to get a job and to support underprivileged groups and poor people in forming self-help concepts for a better future. Altogether, the Economic-Opportunity-Program cost about $ 1 billion. In 1965, the Public Works and Economic Development Act provided regions with a high unemployment rate or a low average family income with $ 665 million. Unfortunately, the bigger part of the money did not benefit the poor; most of it got stuck within the workings of bureaucracy. (Wynn 413)

It may strike one as surprising that, at the same time, revolutions were developing within black parts of the population because after all, as Heath stresses, Kennedy and Johnson had been more concerned with putting an end to racial discrimination than any other president before. Heath speculates that black citizens probably came to feel neglected; a situation that may have escalated due to the increasing U.S. participation in Vietnam, which quickly came to overshadow other important political goals (12). However, as for the black civil rights movement, which came to be known as the 'Black Power Movement' in 1966, following Stokely Carmichael's demand for 'black power' meaning active resistance, Johnson succeeded in convincing Congress to finally pass a bill already drafted by Kennedy. Its purpose was to stop discrimination against African-Americans. These were now, among other things, guaranteed measures concerned with the abolishment of segregation in schools and the prevention of racial discrimination in public institutions. Yet when Martin Luther King, initiator of the peaceful black protest movement in the late 1950s, was murdered in 1968, race riots reemerged. This was primarily due to a white man, James Earl Ray, being strongly suspected of having committed the crime. At the very end of the decade though, the 'negro revolt' slowly lost its impact. Various other protest movements which had emerged during the previous years such as the more radical black nationalist movement led by Malcolm X, died down soon after King was buried. But still, only by judging from the plurality of emerging organizations like CORE with their boycotts and sit-ins, the significance of the 1960s for what came to be called the African American Civil Rights Movement becomes evident.

At this point, another fight for equal treatment deserves mentioning. The Mexican-American or Chicano Civil Rights Movement of the 1960s also demanded equality and further the recognition of the Mexican-American ethnic culture. The movement arose from various forms of negative stereotyping such as discrimination and second-class citizenship. In the end, the protests achieved that residential segregation and discrimination became illegal during that decade (Kutler 464). Particularly with regard to this chapter's focus on political, social, and cultural change processes in the U.S., it is further important to note that the Mexican-American or Chicano Civil Rights Movement naturally added new challenges to the concept of American national identity.

In this context, it is also vitally important to remember that since Kennedy's presidency, when the African American Civil Rights Movement had been reinforced due to incidents such as the assassination of the leader of the NAACP and bomb attacks on black parts of the American population, the atrocities and the social injustice were broadcasted via television. This essentially contributed to the rise in international awareness and protest, so that both the nation and the world expected the U.S. government to give matters of racial equality top priority. In continuing what Kennedy had begun, Johnson successfully met these demands, but his 'War on Poverty' had proven a failure. Only less than 1% of the GNP had been granted to fight poverty and the myriad of measures, however well-intentioned they may have been, created little more than confusion, organizational difficulties, and waste (Wynn 417). Nevertheless, all things considered, Neil A. Wynn, professor of 20th-century American history, regards the war in Vietnam as the deathblow of the 'Great Society' (ibid). In order to wage a war which was as futile as it was expensive, the government reduced expenses for its reformative efforts and had to put up with a split in society which would remain unparalleled until more than thirty years later in response to the Iraq War.

The large-scale involvement of U.S. armed forces in Vietnam is oftentimes interpreted as a reaction to the so-called Gulf of Tonkin Incident, but Wynn positions it in a broader context arguing that the U.S. getting involved in the war in Vietnam must be seen as the inevitable consequence of America's foreign policy following World War II (ibid). As a supporter of Eisenhower's 'Domino Theory,' Kennedy had been persuaded of the necessity of containment and so was Johnson. In addition, as Wynn points out, both of them tended to see world politics in its general concept as a fight between communism and democracy. Cultural differences were dangerously ignored and sometimes it seemed even worthwhile to support dictatorial regimes such as President Batista's regime on Cuba. These decisions were built on a fear that communists might come into power militarily and financially. Wynn therefore concludes that the Vietnam War eventually resulted from the fear of being unable to confine the influence of left forces by providing economic aid, so that the U.S. saw violent intervention as the only possibility to maintain its self-appointed position as 'world policeman.' After Kennedy had sent the first American troops to South Vietnam in order to support the Diem regime, he tragically mistook nationalists and anti-colonialists for communists and largely ignored the fact that what he was dealing with was, in fact, a civil war. (Wynn 417-19)

When Johnson took office, he was regarded as the "peace candidate," but then again, he had never been strictly opposed to fighting the Vietcong (Heath 226). Soon he kept making similar mistakes as to disregard the guerrilla tactic of the enemy, which made conventional warfare impossible. Johnson chiefly counted on material and numeral superiority, and in 1964 he was equipped with even almost plenary powers. During his presidency, the U.S. involvement increased rapidly and so did the number of deployed soldiers. While the government documented 147 dead soldiers in 1964, 14,500 lost their lives only four years later with 93,000 being wounded. In 1967, the annual amount the government spent on the war added up to $ 28 Billion and one year later the costs amounted to 56% of the federal budget, while Congress began to cut funds for domestic measures. (Wynn 419-420)

2.3 Rebelling or 'Dropping Out'? – The Counter Culture of the 1950s and 1960s

Meanwhile, the war atrocities shown on TV caused a storm of indignation throughout the country. When American journalists famously revealed that hundreds of unarmed civilians, women, and children had been killed in My Lai by American soldiers because they could not be distinguished from troops, the faith in the abilities of government to judge the winning prospects diminished drastically; it was clear that the war had gotten out of control.

In response to the ubiquitous notion of futility and due to the ceasing identification with the government, the campus revolts starting around 1965 were oftentimes referred to as, in Stanley I. Kutler's words, "the most sustained, dramatic protests against the Vietnam War" (481). Among those, the big protest march on the Pentagon, which took place in October 1967, doubtlessly caused the biggest stir and most impressively reflected the strong disagreement with the U.S. involvement in Vietnam. Being described in detail in Mailer's *The Armies of the Night*, the novel captures the demonstration's unique spirit and constitutes one of the most valuable cultural 'documents' of the decade.

However, the student anti-war movement already originated in the 1950s when the Eisenhower administration gradually began to set up American soldiers in order to assist the Saigon regime. Back then, the rebelling students were generally referred to as "The Movement." As described by Heath, "The Movement" existed as a rather "loose coalition" of college students, all of whom opposed the war in Vietnam. Their reasons were of course diverse, yet two principal reasons can still be identified as underlying the more specific ones: idealism and the fear of dying in a war which the older generation had decided to wage (Heath 239).

During the 1960s some of the student organizations even set themselves much more extreme goals, as this is illustrated by the plans of the "Students for a Democratic Society" (SDS) to set up a guerrilla troop in 1967. What had begun as a formal organization with activist Tom Hayden writing brilliant speeches which expressed his generation's helplessness but also criticized anti-communism as an ideology and identified capitalism as the root of all evil, radicalized steadily (ibid. 241-42). But also more generally, as Wynn observes, young people started to take more interest in political matters during the 1960s. Almost in accordance with the college students, youngsters demanded radical changes in the government's program, which sometimes even formed revolutionary tendencies. In consequence, the age for eligible voting was not lowered to 18 years until 1971 (Wynn 426).

But still, the function of the (early) anti-war movement as an inducement for the development of several new groupings and movements must not be underestimated. The New Left, for instance, is said to have drawn particular inspiration from more radical acts of liberation and leaders such as the black nationalist movement or South-American revolutionaries (ibid 426). The movement was founded in the late 1950s by a small number of college students and faculty members and was in search of alternative political and social concepts. As Heath specifies and the name already implies, it clearly denied a Marxist-Leninist emphasis on the working class. Instead, it stressed alienation and humanism, referring back to the humanistic socialism of the young Marx and the writings of pacifist and philosophical thinkers (240). In general, the New Left mainly attracted public interest due to its radical attitudes and actions. Sociologist Todd Gitlin refers to that in characterizing the movement as both the core and precursor of the cultural rebellion of the 1960s: "The New Left became the dynamic center of the decade, pushing the young forward, declaring that change was here, forming the template for the revolts of hippies, women, and gays" (4). Still, due to the rather undisciplined character of its members and its skeptical attitude towards leadership, resulting in a lack of proper coordination, the New Left's ever-present task was to strike a balance between duty and anarchy. The movement's image thereby perfectly came to suit the image of one of its most prominent members: Norman Mailer.

In the context of the anti-war movement another development calls for special attention: It is interesting to observe that the population began to split up into different groups in a way that simultaneously paralleled and opposed the unifying character of the anti-war euphoria; the 'counter-culture' of the 1950s and 1960s was born. Among several groups, especially those named in the following allow for the term 'counter culture,' defined by sociologist Douglas Kirby as "a semi-organized culture which examines and challenges many political and non-political features of the dominant culture" (203).

As the use of drugs increased among American soldiers in Vietnam and provided, ironically speaking, the safest way of escaping reality, so did drug abuse in many parts of the American society. Primarily for the so-called 'hippies,' drugs played an essential role in the search for an alternative life style as LSD, marihuana, and even heroin were in daily use. In *Acid Dreams* (1985), their detailed analysis of the significance of drugs in the sixties, Martin A. Lee and Bruce Shlain interpret the use of drugs as conveying two messages: On the one hand, it was a "way of saying 'No!' to authority" as it was an illegal act; on the other hand, it indicated the reborn desire to not only fight social injustice but to return to a "search for personal authenticity" (127-28). Ideologically speaking, the hippies completely disapproved of the system and 'rebelled' quietly in the name of "flower power" and "love-ins," emphasizing emotionality as a concept completely opposing the brutality of war and allegedly rational decisions of the political leaders. Unconsciously or not, in doing so, they in a way also opposed the 'beat attitude' of the fifties, to be elaborated on below. Tracing the development from hipster to hippie, Lee and Shlain note the following: "The new hipsters had cast aside the syndrome of alienation and despair that saddled many of their beatnik forebears. The accent shifted from solitude to communion, from the individual to the interpersonal." (141-42)

Very ironically, the specific, sloppy hippie fashion was quickly adopted by leading fashion houses and soon became *en vogue*. Thus, the intention to visualize a rejection of social norms through a clothing style backfired and became a kind of new fashion norm for the middle class, which Wynn reads as a quaint depiction of the flexibility and vitality of the capitalist U.S. economy (427). Yet it cannot be denied that hippie counter culture entailed a change of norms in many more respects: The young people preoccupied themselves with Asian religions, tolerated premarital sex, and the gay liberation movement began to grow during the late 1960s. In his best-seller *The Greening of America* (1970), Charles A. Reich interpreted this development as an uplift for the U.S. consciousness and predicted a non-violent revolution originating in the very individual and affecting culture first and foremost instead of aiming at an overthrow of the political system (cf. Reich 9). Meanwhile, the larger part of the older generation felt provoked by the looks and attitudes of those youngsters and feared anarchy, apocalypse, and moral decay (Wynn 427).

As touched upon above, the origins of hippie culture can, in turn, be traced back to a specific counter culture of the 1950s: the beat generation. This phrase was coined by U.S. football player and writer Jack Kerouac, who at first exclusively used it to refer to him and his friends "who, he felt, represented a complex of attitudes which existed among the youth across the face of America" (Feldman/Gartenberg 10). Yet he soon became aware that "beatness was not an exclusive condition" (ibid. 11) so that the term 'beat generation' was soon in common use describing "an actual generation that was responding in certain ways to existence in mid-century" (ibid).

According to Wolfgang Riedel, it was the beats whose reaction to what was known as the 'generation gap' became first manifest in counter culture (35). They set out to break sexual taboos as a response to patriarchal family structures and in order to provoke government. Due to the political ideals of the older generation such as the idea of 'massive retaliation,' the core term of rollback, emigration to India or Afghanistan seemed like the last resort for many of them. This paralleled the fact that young conscientious objectors oftentimes fled to Canada or Europe (Wynn 421). For those who stayed, linguistic innovations, most prominently established by Allen Ginsberg, became a – frequently censored – artistic vehicle for protest and counter culture (Riedel 36). Within the grouping of the beats, the so-called 'beatnik' constituted the popular version of the more intellectual beat. Whereas the beats demanded intellectual sincerity and attacked the academic elite of the New Critics (ibid. 39), the beatniks more or less just 'rocked' against what they regarded as an affluent society and turned stars like Bob Dylan – also a dear friend of Ginsberg's and an inspiration to him – and bands like *Grateful Dad* or *Mothers of Invention* into idol-like figures of the counter culture of the 1950s. Those two bands, especially the latter, successfully proved to be capable of conveying the 'beat attitude' through their music and their lyrics in particular. In the *Mothers of Invention*-song *Who Needs the Peace Corps* the lines go: "[...] Think I'll just DROP OUT / I'll just go to Frisco / Buy a wig & sleep / On Owsley's floor [...] / I'm completely stoned / I'm hippy & I'm trippy / I'm a gypsy on my own [...]" (qtd. in Baacke 72) Here, by judging from the capitalization of the phrase "drop out" alone, the significance of the central act of what Gene Feldman and Max Gartenberg describe as "pull[ing] [oneself] out of an increasingly meaningless rat race" (11) and escaping "a game which kills time, deadens awareness and brutalizes feeling" (ibid.) is clearly stressed both audibly and visually. The beats evidently did not wish to be a part of U.S. society. On the contrary, Feldman and Gartenberg adequately sum up the 'beat attitude' in characterizing it as a "rejection of the past and the future, the rebellion against organized authority, the revulsion felt for the Square" (ibid.) and note that, in the written word, "these [attributes] found increasing expression in the works of writers such as Norman Mailer" (ibid.).

And indeed, in his famous essay "The White Negro" (1957), Mailer in some way even provides a specific 'beat vocabulary' by defining key terms such as 'hipster' or 'square' and delineating the concept of 'hip' as constituting both a language and a philosophy of life at the same time (345, 358). In short, to Mailer, the "phenomenon" (343) 'hipster' is personified by "the American existentialist" (ibid) – a man who, knowing that he is facing "a death by *deus ex machina*," (ibid.) has "to live with death as immediate danger," which is why he must "divorce [him]self from society" (344). He is also necessarily a "philosophical psychopath" (348) interested in codifying his innate "desire to rebel" (ibid). His aim is to explore experience (344) and, since this is taking place in a "burning consciousness of the present," (347) to him also "truth is no more nor less than what one feels at each instant in the perpetual climax of the present" (359). Moreover, the hipster constitutes the social opposition to the 'square;' the former rebels, the latter conforms (344). Eventually, the hipster is a "white Negro" for as he has to endure the same marginalization the blacks have had to cope with for centuries (344), the hipster "absorbe[s] the existentialist synapses of the Negro" and so "for practical purposes could be considered a white Negro" (346). To come full circle, Feldman and Gartenberg regard the hipster as "the most advanced Beat Generation type" (12). It is therefore no wonder that it almost feels like quoting Mailer when they continue that "as a consequence, his [i.e. the hipster's] concern is primarily one of self-exploration, of perceiving the self in terms of its connection with immediate experience" (ibid.).

The late 1950s and the 1960s turned out to be years of the extremes. The population found itself torn between trust and a loss of confidence in its leaders. After Kennedy had taken office, his vision of a 'New Frontier' caused a nation-wide euphoria, but in the following years, pessimism came to overshadow the nation. This was both a result of and a reaction to the economic, social, and political development. Some decided to close their eyes in denial, but especially the sixties as a decade shaped by watchwords such as the 'New Frontier' or the 'Great Society' would in collective memory remain the years of disagreement, incomprehension, and depression. Echoing Mailer in "The White Negro" eventually leaves no space for optimism: "These have been the years of conformity and depression. A stench of fear has come out of every pore of American life, and we suffer from a collective failure of nerve." (343)

2.3.1 'Anything Goes' – Mass Culture and Postmodernism

As pointed out before, the turbulent and violent 1960s underwent many changes all of which came to influence America's self-perception immensely. Yet perhaps the most distinct feature of the 1960s remains an increasing modernization and rapidly advancing technology. Meant to make life easier, the modernization of every area of life, however, has come across harsh criticism in scholarly discourse and beyond. In one of the earliest studies of the counter culture and its historical context, *The Making of a Counter Culture* (1969), Theodore Roszak tightly links the youth's discontentment to a phenomenon he names "technocracy." According to Roszak, "technocracy," defined as a "social form in which an industrial society reaches the peak of its organizational integration" (5), is largely responsible for the increasing feeling of alienation the youth tries to rebel against. Although he acknowledges that such "immediate emergencies as the Vietnam war" demand political activism, he clearly decides that "the paramount struggle of our day is against a far more formidable, because far less obvious, opponent [...] 'the technocracy'" (4). The secret of technocracy basically lies in its secrecy. It takes a while to detect this "regime of experts" (7) since people are so used to regarding science as "an undisputed social good" (205). He even goes so far as to put technocracy on a level with totalitarianism "because its techniques become progressively more subliminal" (9). While technocracy rules by "exploiting our deep-seated commitment to the scientific world-view" (ibid.), politicians and scientists sell it as – and here he openly criticizes Johnson's politics – "being 'free,' being 'happy,' being the Great Society" (17). However, at the end of the day, capitalism is again detected to be the underlying nuisance, as Roszak remarks that "the evils stem simply from the unrestricted pursuit of profit" (ibid.).

Simultaneously, mass production and widely homogenous technological forms of entertainment paralleled what came to be termed 'mass culture,' defined by Andreas Huyssen as "the culture of everyday life" (vi) – a socio-cultural phenomenon heatedly debated in its ramifications ever since. Referring to mass culture's tight links to technology, Huyssen documents a "homogenization of difference" (9) and sees the computer as people's "substitute consciousness" (193).[3] As pointed out by Gerhard Hoffmann, in accordance to mass production, cultural trends established by the mass media contributed to a considerably uniform nature of mass culture (b, XI). This is likely to become most apparent when contrasted

---

[3] For an extensive discussion of the decisive role of technology in changing 20th-century art, see Walter Benjamin's essay "The Work of Art in the Age of Mechanical Reproduction" (1935/1936).

with the variety of interests prevailing in the counter culture of the 1960s. In line with that observation, Norman Denzin points to the importance and power of the mass media by concentrating on the visual media, which flourished during the 1950s and 1960s, in order to explore the most complex cultural concept underlying the second half of the 20th century – postmodernism. In his eyes, one can only begin to grasp postmodernism with all its implications – some of which are to be addressed below – if one turns to on-screen-productions which are developed within and therefore might reconstruct or at least draw upon the cultural state of the period as "the search for the meaning of the postmodern moment is a study in looking. It can be no other way. This is a visual, cinematic age" (viii).

Interestingly enough, a lot of cultural critics consider the U.S. to be one of the most postmodern settings. Elaborating on Jean Baudrillard's claim that "the cinema and TV are America's reality" (qtd. in Denzin vii), Denzin, for example, crowns the U.S. "perhaps the most postmodern of contemporary social structures" (vii). Meanwhile, Huyssen even takes the nation's inner conflict between a "powerful sense of the future and of new frontiers" on the one hand and "crisis and generational conflict" on the other hand as a breeding ground for postmodernism, claiming that this specific "historical constellation in which the postmodernism of the 1960s played itself out [...] makes this avantgarde specifically American" (191). Hoffmann holds the same view. In his extensive essay "The Sixties and the Advent of Postmodernism," he clearly presents the American 1960s, which are – like postmodernism – "obviously not a period susceptible to any kind of easy summary" (a, 191), as life-giving to the postmodern. To him, they are "the origin of postmodernism," and postmodernism, in turn, is "the most important result of the sixties" (ibid.). Accordingly, the sixties bequeathed their genes to the postmodern: "The sixties are a composite of contradictory trends, so is postmodernism." (ibid.)

In discussing mass culture and postmodernism with particular consideration of their close entanglement and their connection to the arts and the humanities, Andreas Huyssen's *After the Great Divide: Modernism, Mass Culture, Postmodernism* (1988) provides an illuminating reading of the scholarly exploration of these two highly complex phenomena. Published in the late eighties, the time when the term postmodernism gained its greatest popularity, Huyssen's account is exemplary as it approaches a highly intricate subject by the use of witty and concise language. Therefore, some of his ideas will be referred to in order to elaborate further on the development, the numerous definitions, and the impact of postmodernism. According to Huyssen, postmodernism – being the highly loaded term it is – can only be grasped if one refrains from trying to define it in terms of quality. Discussing the state of research, he sees the tendency "to reduce all cultural criticism to the problem of quality" as "a symptom of the anxiety of contamination" (viii). He thereby alludes to the massive output of new art forms during the 1950s and 1960s, whose distinct feature was a combination of high art and mass culture (ix). In his view, trying to classify postmodernism by the problematic criterion of quality is clearly a "futile attempt" (vii) and thus meant to fail.

Instead, rather than trying to define it as a style, Huyssen thinks it much more fruitful to see the postmodern as a "historical condition" (182). Starting from this, he begins to substantiate his point by 'mapping the postmodern;' he searches for a sort of paradigm shift in order to trace back the origins of postmodernism. Such paradigm shifts are found in the last decades of the 19th century and the first years of the 20th century as well as the two decades following World War II (vii), so that Huyssen finally decides to position the beginnings of postmodernism in the late 1950s continuing up to the eighties (xi). This dating is supported by Hoffmann, who also talks about postmodernism as a "new paradigm" which, at the turn of the sixties, replaced a traditional, restrictive worldview by one emphasizing possibility and freedom (a, 193). In the periods in which Huyssen detects paradigm shifts, he clearly identifies a "discourse which insists on the categorical distinction between high art and mass culture" (vii). Certainly, this "Great Divide," as he terms this discourse pointing to the strict demarcation, must have preceded the paradigm shift which generated the postmodern for a merging of high art and mass culture is in fact a feature – albeit a fairly broad one – critics can concordantly ascribe to postmodernism.

Characteristically, in discussing the Great Divide, one is talking about 'modern(ist)' times. And indeed, as Huyssen claims, "modernism constituted itself through [...] an anxiety of contamination by its other: an increasingly consuming and engulfing mass culture" and insisted on "the autonomy of the art work" while avoiding the culture of everyday life and, thus, political, economic, and social concerns (vi). Since, as argued above, postmodernism was nothing like that but, in fact, completely opposed in its development, one might now be easily tempted to take Huyssen's title *After the Great Divide* as a programmatic answer to one of the most frequently asked questions of the postmodernism debate, namely 'What is 'post' about postmodernism?'. However, the author himself puts a finger on the debate indicating that the prefix 'post' should not be read as 'after' in the sense of timely demarcation from modernism. Although claiming that the Great Divide was replaced by "the paradigm of the postmodern" (ix-x), he explains that this does not equal a total break between modernism and postmodernism. Instead, the two theories must be understood as existing in a "mutual relation" (x) and postmodernism, thus, as a relational phenomenon (183). In insisting that a definition of postmodernism can only derive from modernism, Hoffmann, Hornung, and Kunow support Huyssen's argument (21). Slightly diverging, Susan Sontag holds a more radical view on the role of modernism. She tends to see it as a concept which is clearly inconsistent with postmodernism and is representative of all critics who take "*Antimoderne*" as synonymous with postmodernism (cf. Hoffmann b, XVIII). Although new 'paradigm' might be after all too strong a word, Huyssen's argument remains the most convincing one. Why else should modernism be referred to in post*modernism* if not to imply that it is still reflected within what he calls a new paradigm? Consequently, the prefix 'post' is rather a reference point than a sign of timely succession.[4]

Stressing the crucial importance of a consideration of modernism, Huyssen broadly defines postmodernism as "a challenge in this century to the canonized high/low dichotomy" (vii). This goes in line with what has by now become a common assumption in cultural studies, namely that thinking in binaries should be avoided. In fact, it is even hard to imagine what a binary account of postmodern art would look like since the object to be scrutinized is itself generally "diverse and multifaceted" (Huyssen x). Evidently, "the boundaries between high art and mass culture have become increasingly blurred" (ibid. ix) so that the "postmodern condition in literature and the arts" (ibid.) is essentially characterized by an amalgamation of cultural forms due to a clear artistic trend to incorporate mass cultural and high cultural forms in one piece of art, be it a picture, a book, or any other work of art (ix).

The question remains how postmodernism as a cultural theory and concept is expressed in practice and thus, in turn, simultaneously 'defined' *by* the works of art that develop within it. Unquestionably, the term 'postmodernism' does indeed lead in many directions and must be understood in an interdisciplinary fashion: As summed up by Denzin, it has as yet been used in order to refer to "a movement called postmodernism in the arts," "historical transformations that have followed World War II," and also "social, cultural, and economic life under late capitalism" (3). But it seems that an appropriately extensive first idea can in fact be evoked by means of concrete examples and an involvement of further scholarly positions. For instance, one well-known example of postmodern expression in the arts is 'pop art,' which had its heyday during the 1960s and primarily took up everyday culture and consumer-related themes. Two pioneers of this art form, Roy Lichtenstein and Andy War-

---

[4] This discussion is highly reminiscent of the debate which evolved around the term post(-)colonialism. Significantly, nowadays, post(-)colonial theorists generally include the period of colonization when talking about post(-)colonialism.

hol, once described pop art as "anti-contemplative, anti-nuance, anti-mystery" (qtd. in Riedel 34), which conveys a notion of this art – or rather artists – to be emphasizing intuition and a sense of reality as strictly – hence the anti – opposed to deliberation and vagueness.

Equally important, in line with the deconstruction of hierarchical structures in the art sector, also in the literary sector modern elitist boundaries between 'high literature' and 'popular literature' were traversed; the novel was becoming 'popularized.' In practice, this meant that the fusion of high literature and popular literature caused the "'serious' novel"[5] soon to function as a playful medium in which authors revisited traditional subjects, reworked known rhetoric, stylistic, and discursive devices, and dared to rewrite popular genres like the detective novel, the Western, or Science Fiction. Accordingly, the 'New Fabulators' – named after Robert Scholes' work *The Fabulators* (1967) – created distinctly intuitive, surreal worlds and incorporated elements of magical realism in their works, revisiting older narrative forms such as fantasy, myth and – as Scholes' term suggests – fable. Literary scholars regard this reorientation primarily as an effect of the inability and an indication of the unwillingness to deal with an atrocious reality. "[A]s fiction lost confidence in its power to encompass the world and reach an audience" (Dickstein 20), novelists increasingly incorporated fantastic elements in their works. Two prime examples for this are Pynchon's choice to create in Herbert Stencil, the (anti-)hero of his novel *V.* (1963), a character with a "forcible dislocation of personality" (McHale 22), puzzled and aloof like the contemporary world, or William Burroughs' imaginative distortions of reality in *Naked Lunch* (1959). For some writers, it evidently seemed inappropriate, even impossible to produce prose that featured stories which would take place in an ideal world or which would even stick to the conventions of literary realism. Ultimately, "[t]he incompatibility of the real and the ideal may be one reason why postmodern fiction shifted its adventures into the space of the imaginary" (Hoffmann a, 199).

With his critically acclaimed essay "Cross the Border – Close that Gap: Post-Modernism" (1969), American literary theorist and critic Leslie Fiedler is generally considered to have introduced postmodernism into literary studies. In his text, he traces back and applauds the way postmodern literature subverts the hitherto existing hierarchy of a canonized body of 'literature.' Further, the author, a literary theorist and critic himself, also makes a strong case for a necessary approximation of literary criticism to the postmodern vocabulary of the new generation of writers,

---

[5] In his essay "Cross the Border – Close that Gap: Post-Modernism" (1969) Leslie Fiedler argues that the "'serious' novel," meaning the Art Novel, is outdated due to the impact of 20th-century technology and philology on literature (334).

intending that "the situation of American letters at the end of the sixties" (329) would finally be appropriately described. In doing so, his main argument is that modern literature is "dead" (329) so that the modern "Age of Criticism" (330) is also no longer valid. In postmodern times, described by Fiedler as an "age of myth and passion, sentimentality and fantasy" (331) with a disquietly "apocalyptic" (330) tenor to it, "the kind of criticism which the age demands" (332) has to be "comical" and "vulgar" (ibid.) for due to its close preoccupation with art, it is itself a work of art (331).

The author then moves from literary criticism to literature as the actual art form put under scrutiny in order to enhance his argument. As modernism is dead, so is the "Old Novel" (333). Critics have to accept the "absurdity, even impossibility" of this "'serious' novel" defined as "the Art Novel as practised by Proust, Mann and Joyce" and, accordingly, the absurdity and impossibility of "'serious' criticism" (334) as practiced by American literary critics. In contrast, the developing "New Novel" (334) shows a tendency to become explicitly "anti-art" and "anti-serious" (334), which, as noted above, goes in line with the development of pop art in the arts.

Significantly, Fiedler is another influential critic who also refers to the young America. Without the young Americans, he argues, the introduction of postmodernism into literature would not have taken place. They read novels which are "at the furthest possible remove from art and avant-garde" (336) and thereby, implicitly, urge "certain ageing, reluctant critics onwards towards the abandonment of their former elite status" (345). So at the end of the day, there is more to postmodernism than a merging of high and pop cultural forms. "Most importantly of all," Fiedler concludes, "[postmodernism] implies the closing of the gap between artist and audience, or at any rate, between professional and amateur in the realm of art" (345). In order for it to become a valid cultural or literary theory, he argues that an abolishment of hitherto undisputed boundaries between the producer and receiver of a work of art must be acknowledged in literary criticism so that a scholarly discourse about postmodernism can be assured.

At the end of this sketch, it is to consider which of the issues touched upon above are particularly relevant to a discussion of new journalistic works. The idea of a fusion of different art forms and an increasing 'popularization' of literature, for example, is in this context of crucial significance for obvious reasons. As Hoffmann observes, writers made steady use of and referred back to certain reference texts (b, XIX). Such reference texts in new journalistic writing were as unconventional as diverse. In the case of *In Cold Blood*, for instance, Capote based its 'nonfiction novel' on almost countless newspaper articles, interviews, or other forms of 'evidence' which were to serve as pieces of the puzzle. Like in *The Armies of the Night*, the reference texts sometimes were not even 'texts' in the sense of the written word; Mailer chose to deal with the Vietnam War being a "central *'event'*" (Hoffmann a, 195) of the sixties and for the most part relied on his own perception of the march on the Pentagon as the overall subject of his account. Moreover, the emphasis on intertextuality in postmodernism is closely related to Hoffmann's idea of a "postmodernism of hybridity" (a, 204), a "combination of styles" (ibid.) which stems from his approval to divide postmodernism up into different postmodernisms in order to do justice to the term's various definitions. This was most famously suggested by Fredric Jameson in his influential essay "Postmodernism and Consumer Society" (1983) (543). The "playful spirit" (Hoffmann a, 194), the "'anything goes'-attitude" (ibid.), and the negation of a superior/inferior dichotomy further paved the way for the reconsideration of the strict separation of traditional concepts such as fact and fiction, which played a central role in new journalism. As will be highlighted in chapter 2.2.2 and the analyses, the new journalists challenged these notions through their writing techniques as well as the construction of their works and the treatment of their subject matters. Therefore, the questions in how far new journalism is informed by the postmodern "radical break with [...] mimetic aesthetic" (Huyssen 9) and how it, like postmodern art, "not only mirrors life" but "structures and reproduces it" (Denzin x) will be of concern.

2.4 Making up the News – The Coming of 'Faction'

In line with, for instance, Roszak's or Huyssen's criticism of the dominance of technology and the permanent need for advancement, John Hollowell expresses the effect that such a hunger for science had on the information age claiming that "[w]ith the ever-increasing 'knowledge explosion' in our [i.e. American] society, readers have desired news coverage with greater depth and background" (24). Apparently, new journalism arrived in the nick of time. When the new journalists started their experimentation, they may have sensed that the more 'scientific' idea of objective news coverage could no longer be upheld given that their works seemed to be based on, as Nick Nuttall puts it, a "cultural consensus – those texts loosely agreed upon as examples of a journalism distinct from and atypical of the mainstream" (132). But where exactly was journalism heading during the 1960s? And what other mainstreams were there before?

Since this book is concerned with a genre at the borderline between American literary and journalistic work, the changing ideas and ideals in American journalism must not be completely ignored. They will therefore be traced in the following, which means exploring a realm fairly unknown within literary studies. In order to decide on a starting point that keeps this overview to a manageable length, it seems adequately extensive to widen the scope to the 1830s for modern journalism can be seen as originating in the news coverage typical of the penny papers which developed in the course of this decade (Schudson a, 57). This journey back in time is mainly going to focus on the development of the subjectivity/objectivity binary – surely the most common dichotomy in the history of the press. This is done in order to point out potential predecessors of the new journalists of the 1960s as well as to explore what incidences triggered more subjective or objective news coverage respectively. That way, the new journalists' decision to create increasingly personal accounts of reality – be 'reality' interpreted as 'real events' or something that might be called an 'individual truth' – may be grasped more easily.

Finally, the coming of 'faction,' the fusion of fact and fiction in writing, will constitute both the ending point of the journey sketched in the first part of the chapter and the center of the deliberations about to follow in the second part. Put against the background of scholarly debates concerned with the most important aspects of new journalistic writing, the general aim of the second part will be an approximation to the new journalism and the nonfiction novel as well as their generic features. Without this knowledge base, the representations of reality in *The Armies of the Night* and *In Cold Blood* could not be appropriately discussed.

2.4.1 What's the News? – Incidents and Ideals in 19th- and 20th-Century American Journalism

In his study *The New Precision Journalism* (1991), Philip Meyer, former reporter, university knight chair in journalism, renowned author, and overall a luminary in contemporary American journalism, summarizes endlessly repeated complaints about American journalism at the very end of the 20th century as follows: "It misses important stories, is too dependent on press releases, is easily manipulated by politicians and special interests, and does not communicate what it does know in an effective manner" (2). At least in part, this is not only criticism the contemporary (American) journalist has to face. For centuries there have been ongoing debates centering on questions such as what should be regarded as newsworthy or what an allegedly appropriate representation of the news should look like.

But what *did* such representations actually look like in American journalism up to the 1960s when new journalism set in? Back in the 1820s, more than half of the dailies and weeklies had the words "advertiser," "commercial," or "mercantile" in their titles suggesting content devoted to advertising and commercial operations (Schudson a, 17). In contrast, after 1830, other 'telling names' such as "critic," "herald," or "sun" prevailed and indicated a clear shift away from commercial and economic interests towards 'illumination,' a desire to actually inform people (ibid.). Frank Luther Mott, historian of American journalism, even considers it a principal merit of the so-called penny papers "to make newspaper readers of a whole economic class" (241), whereas before a big part of the population had been excluded from getting informed directly and only received the latest news second hand. This significant turn in the history of the American press is termed the "commercial revolution" (Lippmann qtd. in Schudson a, 17), and, as Michael Schudson points out, "established the model which the mainstream of American journalism has since followed" (ibid.). From that time on, one of the new aims was a high circulation. This was enabled by a modernization of the printing process, improvements in transportation and communications, an increasing democratization during the Jacksonian era, and a growing number of people who could read and write (ibid. 31-36, 58). These developments were further accompanied by the editors' emancipation from subsidies from political masters or parties (ibid. 18).

As far as content is concerned, the penny papers added a new facet to what was understood as noteworthy and, thus, newsworthy. Schudson even goes so far as to ascribe to the editors of the penny papers the invention of a new genre "which acknowledged, and so enhanced, the importance of everyday life" (ibid. 26). In what Mott summarizes as the "creed" (242) of these papers, he illustrates the new interest in everyday occurrences as well as the societal changes which were reflected in the rise of the penny press. At that time, local or home-city news, sensational news, and so-called "human-interest" news, defined as "stories of persons who are interesting merely as human beings," gained in importance and led to major changes in the news concept (Mott 243). However, while Michael and Edwin Emery agree on these new policies, they add that already in the 1840s "more and more significant news was creeping into the columns, and the penny papers led in aggressive news gathering" (103). Summing up, the clear shift in American journalism caused by the penny press is echoed in Schudson's words as he adequately personifies these papers as "spokesmen for egalitarian ideals in politics, economic life, and social life through their organization of sales, their solicitation of advertising, their emphasis on news, their catering to large audiences, their decreasing concern with the editorial" (a, 60).

The abovementioned developments are of particular interest since they are said to have formed the basis for an upcoming belief in 'facts' and to have given rise to discourses centering on what should later constitute – but was yet far from being – the ideal in American journalism: objectivity (ibid.). The concept of objectivity and the reliance on facts have been closely intertwined ever since these topics appeared on the agenda. One requires the other; they are inseparable. However, what still today passes for a basic journalistic doctrine was not even an issue until the 1830s since before, as Schudson explains, "American newspapers were expected to present a partisan viewpoint, not a neutral one" (ibid. 4). As this way of thinking slowly diminished due to the democratization in the Jacksonian era described before, historians of American journalism searched for an incident which paved the way for the establishment of the ideal of objectivity. Many of them concluded that the ideal of an objective news coverage kicked in with the rise of the New York Associated Press. In its beginnings, this association consisted of six important papers, originated in 1848, and pursued the plan to take advantage of the transmitting speed of the telegraph by acquiring one telegraphic transmission for all members. That way, news was gathered and could then be sold on to other papers. Since these papers all had widely different political commitments, the scope of the gathered news did not only have to be broadened, the reporting also had to be 'made objective' in order to be acceptable to the clientele (Mott 251, Schudson a, 4). However, as Schudson convincingly argues, one has to keep in mind that the Associated Press was an institution which acted out of self-interest (a, 4-5). It may have first come up with the idea of objective news, but the fact that it made its reporting more objective by avoiding partiality did not automatically establish objectivity as a common professional ideal; business endeavor must not be confused with professional conviction.

As journalism was a fast moving industry already in the 19th century, it is no wonder that the tide turned again only a few years later. Far from what can be considered objective reporting, newspaper content came to be heavily dependent upon sensationalism – "the emphasis on emotion for its own sake" (Emery 95). Generally speaking, the newspapers of the 1880s and 90s featuring sensationalism followed the *New York World*, which itself best exemplifies the new practices. After Joseph Pulitzer had bought this paper in 1883, he did not only tie in with the democratic aspirations of the penny papers as his motto was "I want to talk to a nation, not a select committee" (qtd. in Emery 175), but also, as Mott puts it, "upset the *status quo* and furnished a new formula for the metropolitan daily" (436). This new formula may be brought down to six explicit factors which contributed to its success: The use of the telegraph and the cable for sensational, gossipy, and oftentimes trivial news, so-called publicity "stunts" which aimed at attracting people's attention, a re-evaluation of the editorial in which liberal ideas were expressed, a doubling in pages, a growing use of illustrations, and a promotion which was characterized by boastfulness and self-praise (ibid. 436-39). The *World* owed its success to its publisher's correct assessment of the climate surrounding an increasing urbanization. The unheard-of emphasis on entertainment clearly "responded to the changing experience, perceptions, and aspirations of urban dwellers" (Schudson a, 102). During that time newspapers "benefited from the experience of city life as a spectacle, and they contributed to it" (ibid. 105).

Interestingly enough, on account of its highly innovative practices, this impending newspaper style came to be called the New Journalism. Of course, the term alone gives good reason to search for parallels to the homonymous movement of the 1960s. And indeed, already back in the 1880s journalists wrote literature and published their works in leading newspapers. This process was at least as important as actual news coverage. Schudson states that "at the end of the century there was as much emphasis in leading papers on telling a good story as on getting the facts. [...] Reporters sought as often to write 'literature' as to gather news" (ibid. 5). To stick with the example of the *World*, Pulitzer was one of the first editors to establish this trend and kept putting it forward by, for example, setting up whole women's pages with Romantic fiction and poetry.

However, like the penny papers, the New Journalism of the 1880s was not all about sensationalism. As much as the sensational stunts and stories of the *World* may have contributed to the rise of the yellow press, the paper was also characterized by a very accurate news coverage which expressed Pulitzer's "high-minded conception of a newspaper's role" (Emery 169) and paved the way for informational journalism. To some extent, the *World* even anticipated a sense of objectivity which was to develop shortly after the paper's heyday and emphasized a news policy based on "clarity and brevity" expressed by the so-called "'inverted pyramid' style" (Emery 178). Mott makes this clear by evaluating the different types of reporting. According to him, significant news was the "backbone of the paper" whereas exciting news mainly served to attract a wider readership and "to enliven the paper" (436). However, regardless of its disposition, the paper always enjoyed great popularity. Already after 1887 sensationalism in the *World* diminished drastically, but the paper continued going fast (ibid.).

At the turn of the century, the *New York Times* conquered the pole position – a paper which is still today regarded as the hallmark of

American journalism. The *Times*, in contrast to the *World*, completely abandoned stories and emphasized informational content in order to attract readers of good standing (Schudson a, 5). Like the Associated Press in 1848, fifty years later the *Times* chiefly counted on factual news, but, again, not for idealistic reasons. Only this time the editors felt it was a necessary thing to do in order to appeal to the upper class.

In fact, it was not until the 1920s that objectivity was agreed on due to a changing attitude towards journalism on the part of the journalists as opposed to former opportunistic motives of the editors. During that time distrust of the integrity of government and changes in the way the world was seen eventually served as incentives to let reporters reflect on how they could ensure reliable reporting. Following the experience of propaganda during World War I, journalists came to believe they reported on a reality that political parties had constructed in their own interests and that therefore could no longer be taken for the 'truth' as such. This idea was further enhanced by sociologists claiming that not only politicians, but indeed each individual creates his or her own reality. As a response to this new way of thinking, new journalistic genres such as the political column and the signed news story emerged, explicitly acknowledging a personal way of reporting through the by-line (Schudson a, 6-7, 144-145). Subjectivity therefore came to be equated with expressing 'values' understood as "an individual's conscious or unconscious preferences for what the world should be" which are "ultimately subjective and so without legitimate claim on other people" (ibid. 5-6).

But there was yet another reaction to the feeling that so-called 'facts' could no longer be trusted light-heartedly given that they were no longer regarded as "stand[ing] beyond the distorting influences of any individual's personal preferences" (ibid. 5). As a counterpart to subjective reporting, journalists imposed on themselves an "allegiance to rules and procedures," which operated under the name of "objectivity" (ibid. 7). Very reminiscent of Roszak's gloomy account of the ubiquitous dominance of "technocracy" mentioned in chapter 2.1.2, Schudson suggests that "objectivity seemed a natural and progressive ideology for an aspiring occupational group *at a moment when science was God*" (b, 82, my italics). Interestingly enough, objectivity in science already constituted a leading notion which required a common consensus on an assertion before this assertion was called a fact. In accordance, a journalistic understanding of objectivity from this day forth entailed that "a person's statements about the world can be trusted if they are submitted to established rules deemed legitimate by a professional community" (Schudson a, 7). Thus, facts came to be conceived of as "consensually validated statements about [the world]" (ibid.). In the wake of this increasing "self-conscious professionalism" (Schudson b, 82), the first nationwide professional association of newspaper editors, the American Society of Newspaper Editors, in 1922/23 made the ideal of objectivity official by declaring in its "Canons of Journalism" that "[n]ews reports should be free from opinion or bias of any kind" (Pratte qtd. in ibid..). Ultimately, objectivity was established for noble reasons.

According to Schudson, by the 1960s objectivity had risen to the "emblem of American journalism" (a, 9). Paradoxically, once fully established, objectivity was challenged more than ever before. While nobody ever doubted that "the idea of objectivity was at the heart of what journalism has meant in th[e] country" (ibid. 10), government management of the news after World War I and II made journalists uneasy. This feeling hit its peak when the war in Vietnam set in and governmental control over the press was still strict. Thus, the sixties should not solely remain the decade in which the youth protested against its authorities; a group of young journalists and writers struck out in equal measure in order to wage a war using pens as their weapons. At first, it was sensed that, in the wake of World War I and II, journalists needed to hold on to objectivity because "they [...] were forced by ordinary human aspiration to seek escape from their own deep convictions of doubt and drift" (ibid. 159). At the end of the day, however, the skepticism increased and numerous journalists and writers, among them the new journalists of the 1960s, even found themselves 'rewriting' their own profession.

2.4.2 The New Journalism and the Nonfiction Novel – What are we talking about?

Many terms synonymously refer to what John C. Hartsock carefully calls "a body of writing that [...] reads like a novel or short story except that it is true or makes a truth claim to phenomenal experience" (1) and what is referred to as new journalism in this study. While such a multitude of terms indicates efforts of the critics to name what is at the heart of this elusive form of writing at the borderline between American journalism and literature, many of them fail to do so precisely because the form is so multi-faceted. It goes without saying that each technical term favors certain aspects and neglects others, but in this case some neologisms like, for instance, "art-journalism [or] essay-fiction" (Weber qtd. in Hartsock 4) appear to be particularly unsuitable. As for the first term, it is unclear which art is being referred to and the second term excludes all works which are not penned in essay form. Others like "journalit" (ibid.) appropriately try to bridge the gap between journalistic and literary writing but have only been used sporadically.[6]

Evidently, there has been and still is a general discomfort surrounding these different nomenclatures. Frustrated after a fruitless attempt to come up with an appropriate term, W. Ross Winterowd even goes so far as to call the texts he refers to the "other" literature (qtd. in ibid. 5). Significantly, in indicating total estrangement and exoticism, the notion of the Other is something we thought to have overcome long ago. In adopting Thomas B. Connery's use of "form" (qtd. in ibid. 3) instead of talking about "genre," Hartsock finally moderates such radical views as that of Winterowd but not without pointing to the fact that even forty years after the first new journalistic works were written, "our understanding of [such texts] is still very much emerging" (ibid.).

Paradoxically, it is exactly this taxonomical uncertainty that lets Wolfe's phrase "new journalism" appear so convincing. In the face of pure intricacy, this term comes in handy for several reasons: To begin with, the term has been widely established in scholarly discourse. Being highly reminiscent of the new journalism of the 1880s, it further makes sense to revive the term as it already in the 19th century denoted an interaction between literature and journalism. The fact that the *new* journalism of the 1960s is, of course, not as unprecedented in its disposition as the new journalism of the 19th century may have been, to be elaborated on below, might at first sight constitute a convincing argument against the use of the term. However, by indulging in discussions about the not-so-new newness of the term,[7] such critical voices tend to neglect that this form of writing was not established by editors, like in the case of Joseph Pulitzer but emanated from bold experimentation of the journalists and writers themselves. They came to doubt the doctrine of objectivity and searched for new ways to write about contemporary reality. This was definitely a novelty. Abiding by Wolfe's term therefore means that the journalistic origin of the movement is acknowledged and commemorated. Besides, there is a certain degree of authenticity to it. Critics, as Hartsock explains, have generally been prone to name these works whose authors make a factual claim but use fictional techniques according to their own affiliation with English studies or journalism respectively (6). But, as it was introduced by Tom Wolfe, a journalist *and* writer, new journalism is not a term 'forced' on the form by critics who may not always be able to relate to what they are commenting on to the same degree that someone can who is involved in its creation. Given these reasons, Wolfe's "new journalism" eventually constitutes an appropriate

---

6   For more terminology see, for example, Hartsock 4-5 and Hollowell 15.
7   Even Wolfe himself agrees that "new" is a somewhat problematic formulation (cf. Wolfe 57-68).

umbrella term which is broad enough to cover a variety of works all of which read like fiction and claim truth but may take on slightly different forms.

Considering that, as mentioned in the introduction, numerous writers made extra money by working as journalists in the past centuries, it is hardly surprising that even long before the 1960s the boundaries between literary and journalistic writing often started to blur in works of writers who held both positions. While journalistic aspirations were generally considered inferior to pursuing a career in literature, some American writers even gained fame despite – or maybe also because of – their heterogeneous style. Therefore, it is valid to perceive writers such as Henry James, Stephen Crane, Mark Twain, Ernest Hemingway, John Dos Passos, or John Steinbeck generally as predecessors to the new journalists of the 1960s (Hollowell 34, Haack 128). Among the examples of 'old new journalistic writing,' with Daniel Defoe's *A Journal of the Plague Year* (1722), one of the most frequently mentioned ones stems from English literature. Comparable to Mailer's *The Armies of the Night*, Defoe's account of the Great Plague of 1665 reads like an eyewitness report. Yet the big difference is that Defoe's report is purely fictive as it was written more than half a century after the event being reported took place, whereas Mailer actually did participate in the march on the Pentagon in 1967. Defoe's account therefore remains "fiction masquerading as fact" (Hollowell 33), which actually reverses the most prominent characteristic of new journalistic works, namely to read like fiction but make a truth claim. A precursor in the form of a literary genre can be found in the autobiography which already began to develop in the 18th century. One well-known example is Mark Twain's *Life on the Mississippi* (1883). Significantly, since autobiographies are necessarily told from the author's point of view, many new journalists chose to write in an "autobiographical format" (Wolfe 58). This of course contributed strongly to a notion of new journalism as a highly "'subjective' journalism" (ibid.) or literary form respectively.

And still, despite all the similarities to older genres, other than the fact that it originated among the journalists themselves, people crying out loud "The bastards are making it up!" (ibid. 24) suggested that there was something really striking about new journalism's increased appliance of fictional techniques to accounts of real-life events. But what exactly was it? As mentioned in the introduction, Tom Wolfe famously claimed that new journalism was "more spectacular in terms of style." John Hollowell's convincing argument that the innovation consisted in the reinforcement and refinement of the extent and degree to which the aforementioned predecessors – more subconsciously than intentionally – "fictionalized" (10) their journalism illuminates Wolfe's remark. According to Hollowell, the new journalists were particularly inventive in that they were "using fictional techniques in more complex and sophisticated ways than did their predecessors" (46-47). Besides, they did so very consciously because the ultimate effect they were trying to achieve was to "use novelistic techniques in order to provide greater psychological depth" (ibid. 47).

As the postmodern reality of the 1960s turned out to be inaccessible by means of either purely fictional or purely journalistic writing, the fact that novelists and writers started to approach each other's domains demonstrated an attempt to hoist an increasingly blurry reality by its own petards. Significantly, an entirely mass-media journalistic account of the atrocities experienced since the early 1960s did no longer seem authentic. As John Hellmann observes, the mass media was prone to present serious incidents such as Kennedy's assassination in an inadequate manner, namely "in formulas of simple conflict and melodramatic action drawn from its fictional entertainments" (2). Neither was the most conservatively objective newspaper journalism as practiced by pursuing the 'inverted pyramid' pattern capable of capturing such an elusive reality. As Nicolaus Mills points out, "[a] who, what, where, when, why style of reporting could not begin to capture the anger of a black power movement or the euphoria of a Woodstock" (xvii). At the same time, however, literary scholars agree that a purely fictional approach in the tradition of literary realism also failed to live up to the present "unique shift in American culture" (Hellmann 2). As "everyday 'reality' became more fantastic than the fictional visions of even [America's] best novelists" (Hollowell 3), new journalism shared its "dissatisfaction with the assumptions of the realistic novel" (ibid. 17) with other literary forms of the 1960s such as Barth's or Pynchon's revived myths or fables. Yet the new journalists regarded it as essential to continue to write about everyday matters. Considering that the specific conventions and techniques applied in the fiction of literary realists in the 19th century "developed [...] to enable the writer to describe the *typical* experience of members of large classes in society" (Hellmann 9), it suggested itself to diverge from the realist tradition. After all, in the 1960s nothing was "typical," common, or representative anymore. With regard to language and writing, a preference of shouting slogans over more elaborated forms of discussion, which Chris Anderson terms the "rhetorical crisis" of the sixties (101), even foreboded radical change. At the end of the day, it dawned on journalists and novelists alike that neither mass-media journalism nor conventional journalism nor realist fiction accomplished to satisfactorily convey contemporary experience.

However, as fictional techniques were still conceived of as essential to provide for the aforementioned "psychological depth," the search for a "form more closely attuned to the altered nature of reality in America than the conventional realistic novel" (Hollowell 14) began. This search came to an end when the new journalists decided to distinctly join together literary fiction and journalism, both of which had traditionally been associated with certain concepts of truth, in order to arrive at what new journalist Gay Talese calls "a larger truth" (vii). Clearly, by fusing journalism and literature, the new journalists came to profit from both forms. On the one hand, the bold venture to approach real life matters regardless of how elusive they might appear made them construct their works on a factual basis. This journalistic spirit replaced the conventions of realist fiction in that "[i]t overcame the weaknesses of the traditional fictional contract, in which the author promised plausibility, by replacing it with a journalistic one promising factuality" (Hellmann 19). On the other hand, as the individual experience and the need for psychological depth were essential, fiction proved to be "the type of writing that provide[d] the most effective means of dramatizing the complexities and ambiguities of experience – the dynamic and fluid wholeness of an event as it [was] felt and ordered ("made") by a human consciousness" (ibid. 18); fictionalizing enabled the account to live up to the author's personal experience.

'Faction,' the pun on the fusion of fact and fiction, is in this context often used as an overall term highlighting these two essential features of new journalistic works. Until the 1970s, when scholars started to examine the new journalism of the 1960s, the term faction had exclusively circulated in its original meaning as a "small group within a large group" (Haack 127). But with regard to what Dietmar Haack calls an increasing "*Faktographie*" in the U.S. in the second half of the 20th century, indicating writing that focused on recent events (ibid.), even in its original meaning, faction in a way already was a telling name. As stated before, only a relatively small group of writers among the vast array of American authors showed interest in a truthful approach to contemporary affairs. However, also in the early 1970s literary scholars had not yet appropriated the term as an indicator of the intermingling of fact and fiction. On the contrary, as Haack shows, at that point in time, the focus was on 'fact,' signifying an interest in real life matters (ibid.). And still, mistrust of the mass media which becomes apparent in this increasing desire to 'investigate' on one's own (ibid. 142) already echoed an important part of what the new journalists expected from the journalistic features of their works. At a time when the mass media could not be trusted due to governmental control, writers had to take the initiative and 'report' on their own. During the late 1970s, however, and especially from the 1980s on, when the term became more widely used, faction eventually came to be understood as a term indicating the amalgamation of two realms which had hitherto been kept apart fairly strictly – factual and fictional discourse. Thenceforward, the fact that the term finally came to broadly designate any form of writing that was "making a claim to reflecting a world of 'fact'" while "acknowledging its relationship to fiction" (Hartsock 1) shows that the fictional components of such texts had won recognition. While, as Horst Zander points out, in some cases it "remains unclear whether ['factional' texts] present a basically factual discourse that incorporates fictional strategies or a basically fictional discourse that adopts the conventions of factual texts" (3), the aim of such texts is mostly considered "to demonstrate the fictionality of factual discourse or even of reality as such" (ibid.). This new perspective raised a lot of questions in academic circles. Most frequently, the highlighting of the dramatizing quality of fiction, which accompanied the shift in perception and which had proven so fruitful in terms of approaching the abovementioned "larger truth" in new journalistic writing, fueled discussions about to what extent the "meaningful versions of the 'news'" that "the authors attempt[ed] to 'make up' or construct" (Hellmann x) were fictional or factual. Deriving from this, the most troubling question at issue soon was 'Is new journalism rather a genre of journalism or fiction?'.

In general, scholarly opinions diverge, but a tendency towards an affirmation of a literary status of new journalistic works can be accounted for. However, as might be expected, the probably most prominent defense of a journalistic disposition comes from Philip Meyer, a central figure in American journalism and journalism studies. Although Meyer does acknowledge the literary features of new journalism, calling them – quite pragmatically – "the literary tools of fiction" (5), he regards new journalism as a subjective kind of journalism "which freed journalists from the constraints of objectivity" (ibid.). He argues that those journalists are granted an "artistic license to become story-tellers" but ultimately create "*journalistic* products that are a joy to read" (ibid., my italics). Interestingly enough, though, he in a way ends up echoing Gay Talese's vision of a "larger truth" as he characterizes new journalism as "an interesting effort at coping with information complexity and finding a way to communicate essential truth" (ibid.).

Literary scholars, on the other hand, try to prove the literariness of new journalistic works in different ways. Drawing on Robert Scholes' discussion of the origins of the key terms 'fact' and 'fiction,' one argument of particular interest is, for example, put forward by John Hellmann, one of the few scholars who wrote extensively on new journalism. Scholes argues that the relationship between the two terms is "artificially dichotomized" (Hellmann 17). Noticing that fact and fiction derive from the Latin verbs 'facere' and 'fingere' meaning 'to make or do' and 'to make or shape' respectively, he challenges the associations between 'fact' and "truth" and 'fiction' and "falsehood" (ibid. 17-18). If fact and fiction are both "made," they are both constructs that differ according to the person who "makes" and "shapes." In an attempt to point out the impact of this observation on new journalistic works, Hellmann argues that the common notion of facts as Schudson's "consensually validated statements" mentioned before, which paved the way for the ideal of objectivity, is no longer valid. Therefore, Hellmann is representative of those theoreticians who maintain that "new journalism is a genre of fiction" (Hellmann 21) and who are consequently more interested in the "aesthetic form and purpose" (ibid. 23) of new journalistic writing than in its "factual subject matter" (ibid.). Peter Bruck and Morris Dickstein hold similar views. Bruck claims that the new journalist understands reality as a product which arises from individually shaped imagination and experience (161), and Dickstein stresses the need to "dramatize" experience (4) if one wants to explore the "psychological effects" the 'unreal' reality has on the individual (17). Tom Wolfe of course also did not miss joining in the debate. Even before he explains how the feature writers set out to take over the domain of the once so respected novelists and argues that reporting is a feature of all storytelling, he already clarifies in the preface of *The new journalism* that the main point of his volume is to show that "the most important *literature* being written in America today is [...] in the form that has been tagged, however ungracefully, the New Journalism" (11, my italics).

However, as *The Armies of the Night* and *In Cold Blood* have both not only been referred to as new journalism but also as 'non(-)fiction novels,' a short negotiation of scholarly views on the nonfiction novel is important. In general, as Dan Wakefield observes, "the negative sound of the term 'nonfiction' always seemed [...] a reflection of the common attitude toward that vast and various field of writing. The term itself indicates that 'fiction' is the standard, central sort of serious writing, and that anything else is basically defined by being 'not' of that genre" (qtd. in Hollowell 59). In a postmodern context, a term like *non*fiction, though trying to work against standardization, implicitly promotes a way of thinking in binaries and seems rather inappropriate. However, in connection to the term 'novel,' the postmodern notion of intermingling becomes obvious at first glance in the phrase 'non(-)fiction novel.' Apart from faction and new journalism yet another phenomenon appeared that indicated hybridity in writing. Still, a definition of the term nonfiction novel indicates its exchangeability with the term new journalism:

> A genre which developed in the 1960s and 1970s, especially in the United States and among writers such as Truman Capote, E.L. Doctorow, Norman Mailer and William Styron. Such novels took real, true, documentary subjects and explicitly represented them

by way of devices associated with narrative diction such as verbatim dialogue, the points of view of a participant/character in the action and detailed description of peoples' clothes, possessions and so forth. (Cobley 237-38)

Accordingly, whenever literary scholars discuss the nonfiction novel, new journalism is also brought up more or less consciously. As might be expected by judging from the definition above, John Hollowell eventually confirms the fact that critics have traditionally used both "genres" (Hellmann 21, Hollowell x) in order to refer to the "new fusion of reporting and fiction" (ix). The two genres are virtually used as synonyms in the same way that nonfiction and journalism are often used interchangeably. This can be seen in the synonymous use of the terms "literary journalism" and "literary non-fiction" (Hartsock 4) or William Wiegand's interpretation of 'nonfiction' as "impl[ying] a willingness to be held responsible for the data included as literally factual" (135), which again stresses that the subject matter is the main thing about the nonfiction novel that is factual.

In accordance, the main characteristics of the nonfiction novel also correspond to those of new journalism. In *The new journalism*, Wolfe lists what he regards as recurrent features of most new journalistic writing. In short, those features are: Scene-by-scene construction, which was to avoid the effect of mere 'retelling;' the recording of full verbatim dialogue regarded as involving the reader more than any other device; detailed research which reinforced the notion of an eye-witness report; a third-person point of view as the most efficient technique to gain access to the mind of every character depicted; and finally, the recording of symbolic details such as everyday gestures or styles of furniture and status symbols which indicate people's place in life (46-47). Wolfe argues that through these components, new journalistic works conveyed a feeling of "'immediacy'" and "'concrete reality'" (ibid. 46). Importantly, in listing new journalism's features, Wolfe was particularly concerned with establishing the genre's close relationship to literary realism (cf. e.g. ibid. 49). In the course of the new journalism debate, this proximity has often been contested. Obviously, judging from the previous deliberations, the diverging and highly individual notions of reality alone naturally prevented the writers from abiding by clear-cut patterns of composition. David Eason convincingly argues that "the term 'realism' is [therefore] not specific enough to be meaningful" and concludes that "an alternative description, one that places the form within the context of culture, is needed" (143).

Thus, a lot has been said about the nature and motivation of new journalism, and Wolfe's affinity towards realism has also been disputed.

However, attempts to classify new journalistic works have mostly been lacking. Therefore, the following analyses constitute a starting point and an incentive for future approaches to a typology by discussing the respective representations of reality to be found in the two novels under scrutiny – novels that have been counted in when it has been claimed that works of new journalism and the nonfiction novel "more than the novels of the sixties […] have served the function of fiction" (Hollowell 11) and achieved to "illuminate[] the ethical dilemmas of [the] time and convey[] the major concerns of these years" (ibid.), but have not been granted individual labeling.

3 Self-Reflexivity as a Path to Personal Truth – Norman Mailer's *The Armies of the Night: History as a Novel, the Novel as History*

Taking a look at the works that precede Norman Mailer's Pulitzer-prize winning *The Armies of the Night: History as a Novel, the Novel as History*,[8] it is hardly surprising that he was soon to become one of the most important new journalists. Virtually ever since Mailer started to write professionally, his works have been concerned with contemporary events and experiences related to the United States of America. His first success *The Naked and the Dead* (1948) even constitutes a first-hand account of the atrocities of World War II experienced by a U.S. company during its fight against Japanese troops, which owed its authenticity to Mailer's decision to voluntarily join the army. Although this literary sensation was followed by two flops, *Barbary Shore* (1951) and *The Deer Park* (1955), those two novels show that the recurrent theme in Mailer's work is a critical examination of American institutions and society. A prime example of Mailer's criticism is the corruption and superficiality of America's flashy and pseudo-spectacular silver screen Hollywood as portrayed in *The Deer Park*. The dry spell of the early and mid-1950s, however, had a positive effect on Mailer's creative output. Making a virtue of necessity, in *Advertisements for Myself* (1959), which is often considered his first nonfiction novel (cf. e.g. Foster 271), he writes about his self-doubts but also recollects his achievements and ambitions as a writer. In combination with some of his earlier stories which he wrote while still a Harvard student, several collected essays, and witty commentaries serving as said 'advertisements' for his works, the book reads like an autobiographical and sometimes even 'therapeutic' study of Mailer's development as an author.

In the 1960s, Mailer turned more and more to writing columns for prestigious U.S. magazines, primarily *Esquire* and *Commentary*. This additional occupation naturally added much to the introduction of a new phase in his literary career which was devoted to a blurring of reporting and writing fiction – to new journalism. "Superman Comes to the Supermarket," a witty report on Kennedy's candidacy, published in *Esquire* in 1960, is often regarded as the origin of Mailer's new journalism. His most noted new journalistic piece "The Steps of the Pentagon," however, was to appear eight years later in a March 1968 issue of *Harper's Magazine* after the editor Willie Morris had suggested to him to write an article

---

[8] In the following, the abbreviation *Armies* will be used.

about the 1967 Washington peace march against the war in Vietnam. Together with his article "The Battle of the Pentagon," published one month later in *Commentary*, *The Armies of the Night* evolved in book form still in the same year. In *Armies*, Mailer combines an account of the march with a prophetic description of suffocating forces in the United States. As it had always been his strategy, he turns those antagonistic forces into subjects of his writing, but, more importantly, also tries out new ways of using the possibilities his profession as a writer offers him in order to express his concerns. Mailer's works, which he considered to be "literary actions" (Gilman 93), ways to move people and make them aware, now even take on the form of "political action" (*Armies* 88). In accordance, literary critic Richard Gilman sums this up very well when he concludes after his assessment of *Armies*: "[T]hat Mailer is only imperfectly a novelist, that his passion for moving and shaking the actual has prevented him from fully inhabiting imaginary kingdoms, is the underlying, paradoxical strength of this book" (151). Significantly, Michael L. Johnson attests the same for the journalistic aspiration of *Armies* by asserting that Mailer creates an "honest, and relevant, if necessarily imperfect, journalism" (70). Such observations apparently led literary critics to reach the consensus that, in Jean Radford's words, "a more contextual treatment may ultimately prove the best way of assessing the literary significance of this particular writer" (2). And Richard Gilman adds: "With no other American writer is it so necessary to keep shuttling between the man and the work [...] because Mailer has made it impossible to separate the two" for he "has lived in public, discharging his personality" (92-93).

Whereas more contextualizing and comprehensive approaches to Mailer's work in general and *Armies* in particular have been predominant, close readings and systematic analyses that focus on specific aspects of his writing have mostly been lacking. With regard to *Armies*, this is probably due to the various topics being touched upon as the anti-war demonstration causes the protagonist Mailer to ruminate about America's general *status quo*. Certainly, it would not be helpful to decide on, exaggeratedly speaking, either close reading as practiced by the New Critics or an emphasis on the historical context of the work in the spirit of the New Historicists. The following analysis therefore generally aims at striking a balance between such approaches. As the focus is on narrative technique, style and figurative language, and the interrelation between form and content, a close examination of significant passages, however, will be of central importance in order to avoid far-fetched discussions and to arrive at an outcome that will provide a fruitful basis for a future typology.

3.1 "Let us then make our comic hero the narrative vehicle' – Self-Reflexivity, Metafiction, and Mailer's Very Own 'Return of the Author'

Doubtlessly, a lot of Tom Wolfe's generalizations about the new journalism and its features can be contested. One thing he is definitely right about, however, is his observation that narrative voice and point of view is "one of the great problems in non-fiction writing" (31). As it is one of the principal goals of the genre to arrive at a 'larger truth,' to supply a truthful report which nonetheless would have to be made up, fictionalized, in order to live up to the fictional quality of reality, one can imagine how hard it must have been to find an appropriate angle from and voice with which the story be told, the event be covered. Wolfe himself, for that matter, was equally flexible and daring. In explaining shifts of point of view that would take place in the blink of an eye by claiming that "this had nothing to do with objectivity and subjectivity or taking a stand or 'commitment' – it was a matter of personality, energy, drive, bravura ... style, in a word" (ibid.), he stresses individual and aesthetic motives. In contrast, stating that "the adoption of the technique of omniscient narration commonly found in realistic novels implies a comprehensiveness of knowledge that many writers refused to accept," Hollowell implies that the tension between objectivity and subjectivity does indeed play an important role in the choice of narrator and point of view (15).

In the case of *Armies*, Mailer's quest for an appropriate style, described by Frank D. McConnell as "not simply a matter of literary, verbal habits but part of a man's whole sense of himself"(64), had an important influence on the narrative technique, as will get clearer in the course of the analysis. However, his personal involvement in the actual event, the protest march, must be considered equally significant because it begs questions about the identity of the narrator and suggests the possibility of an appearance of the real author Norman Mailer. Thus, first, a short survey of some of Mailer's previous choices of narrator and narrative perspective will help to get an idea of how important it is for Mailer to find a narrative technique that he is comfortable with and that best provides a way to cope with contemporary reality.

In *Advertisements for Myself* the commonly agreed on principle of literary theory never to confuse author and narrator, which derives from influential studies like, for example, William K. Wimsatt and Monroe C. Beardsley's essay "The Intentional Fallacy" (1946), is preliminarily suspended as Mailer openly admits that the voice approaching the narratee is he himself. It is at that point of his career, after a decade of encountering harsh criticism for his literary work, that Mailer would write down the following lines, which were to shed light on the narrative technique in this particular book and the works to follow:

> For six years I had been writing novels in the first-person; it was the only way I could begin a book, even though the third-person was more to my taste. Worse I seemed unable to create a narrator in the first-person who was not overdelicate, oversensitive, and painfully tender, which was an off portrait to give because I was not delicate ... (*Advertisements for Myself* 203)

Trying to point out reasons for the immense problems he experienced in writing *The Deer Park* and *Barbary Shore*, he draws the conclusion that the main problem probably lay in the dissimilarity between author and narrator. As a solution to this dilemma, in *An American Dream* (1965) he turns the first-person narrator and protagonist Steven Rojack into an implicit portrait of himself, which he is more comfortable with realizing that his writing would improve if he only "exploit[ed] his own characteristics and ideas, and achieve[d] the unity of vision and voice which was lacking in his second and third novels" (Radford 111). This strategy is slightly modified in *Cannibals and Christians* (1966), where Mailer takes on the roles of an interviewer and an interviewed person named Mailer. By dramatizing a dialogue with himself, he develops a method to confront and question contradictory parts of his self and to reveal the deeper meaning of the most diverse topics occupying his mind such as time, aesthetics, cannibalism, and food.

When Mailer first started to work as a columnist, he was still constantly concerned with the attractiveness of the novel as a literary form. In an article written for *Esquire* in the early 1960s, he describes the novel as a "Bitch Goddess" the novelist sleeps with and then leaves convinced that he just satisfied her every need, whereas she knows about his confidence and even more so about his inability to ever fully satisfy a woman (McConnell 61). However, Mailer is aware of the fact that "a man lays his character on the line when he writes a novel" and that "[s]ome writers are skillful at concealing their weaknesses, some have a genius for converting a weakness into an acceptable mannerism of style" (qtd. in ibid.). Convinced that a novel inevitably reveals the character of the author, but that one can still manage to win this fact for one's own ends, with *Cannibals and Christians* Mailer begins to develop an alternative to past and future concepts that strictly dismiss authorial intention such as "the intentional fallacy" or Barthes' "death of the author." With that in mind, an investigation of the narrative discourse of *Armies*, focusing primarily on two of Gérard Genette's three aspects of narrative discourse, namely the relationship between narrative and narrating and story and narrating (29), promises to be interesting.

Starting off with the identification of the narrative perspective in *Armies*, in Genette's terminology a question of "mood" ("who sees?"), is comparably easier than first trying to answer the question "who speaks?", that is tracing the narrator or Genette's "voice" of the novel (186). At least for the most part, the events taking place before, during, and at the end of the protest march are being reported from the point of view of the main character Norman Mailer as the reader only gets to see what Mailer sees. However, it is not only plainly reported what Mailer sees but also what he thinks while he is seeing something. As experience has always been a crucial issue in Mailer's works, everything does not only happen before Mailer's eyes but rather passes through and has an effect on him. Reacting to what he describes as "the too specifically visual connotations" of the term point of view and its synonyms vision or field (Genette 189), Genette draws upon Cleanth Brooks and Robert Penn Warren's term "focus of narration," which they announced as a synonym for point of view in their study *Understanding Fiction* (1943). In coining the term "focalization" (ibid.), Genette manages to emphasize that the process of regulating information through a character is not only a matter of the character's sight but also of the mind. Subsequently, he classifies several modes of focalization, the most appropriate of which for large narrative sections of *Armies* appears to be "fixed internal focalization" (ibid.), indicating that one never leaves Mailer's viewpoint in these passages and also gets to know about his thoughts.

However, the exception proves the rule. Generally speaking, a lot of 20th-century novels, especially those of early 20th-century modernist literature, very frequently feature sudden shifts in focalization and, thus, in "focal character[s]" (ibid.). In Genette's typology, such concepts of focalization are classified as narratives with variable or multiple internal focalization, depending on whether the perspective shifts from one focal character to a second one or in between more than two focal characters (189-90). *Armies*, however, does neither continuously feature the mode of a fixed internal focalization nor does it shift between fixed and variable or multiple internal focalization. Instead, at some points, the narrative even entirely abandons internal focalization and takes on the form of a "nonfocalized narrative" (Genette 189) in which the events stop passing through Mailer and the plot seems to stagnate. In line with that, this analysis must also stop because in order to explain why and how that happens, the aspect of voice must be included into further deliberations concerned with mood.

With the exception of Book Two, where it is attempted to create a "history" of the march which is also told in the third person but does not focus on any particular character, the story is told in the third person and, as stated in the text, "places its focus on a central figure" (*Armies* 53). This "central figure" and, thus, focal character is, as said before, Norman Mailer, protagonist and "an eyewitness" (ibid.) to the events around him. As Mailer is an eyewitness, the narrator fills the narratee in retrospectively, telling of the people Mailer encounters and the things he sees, as if he had been glancing over Mailer's shoulder when the march took place in October 1967. But, to repeat what has been said before, the narrator does not only report on what Mailer sees but oftentimes also gives an account of Mailer's inner life, his ruminations and associations. This practice might be categorized as free indirect discourse or narrated monologue since the vocabulary of such passages corresponds to that of Mailer which one gets to know in sections of direct speech. The narrator, however, talks in a similar manner, as is best exemplified in passages where the narrator approaches the narratee. It is thus very hard to decide whether it is the narrator describing Mailer's thoughts or an indirect quote of Mailer's thoughts. In such cases, Seymour B. Chatman suggests to speak of a "neutralization" or "unification" of narrator and protagonist (206). However, as it is also reported what Mailer sees and in order not to complicate the matter any further, the point of view or focalization of the larger part of *Armies* is in this analysis generally defined as fixed internal focalization. Strictly speaking, this narrative mode would require that Mailer never be described from the outside and, what is more, that his thoughts never be commented on by the narrator (Genette 192). However, like in the majority of other narratives, this is not the case. It therefore suggests itself, and is also suggested by Genette, to use the term less rigidly (193) so that it is still applicable in *Armies*. In his noted essay "Point of View in Fiction: The Development of a Critical Concept" (1955), Norman Friedman presents and differentiates between eight types of point of view. Among those, the category that comes closest to Genette's fixed internal focalization is "selective omniscience," where "the reader is limited to the mind of only one of the characters" (Friedman 128). This character must be, as can be accounted for in *Armies*, "the fixed center" of the narrative because it is the aim of this narrative perspective "to dramatize mental states" (Friedman 128-29). However, Friedman considers omniscience to cause an "elimination of not only the author," which corresponds to our understanding of all narrative perspectives nowadays, "but also of any narrator whatsoever" (127) – an assertion that no longer matches the views of contemporary narratology. Today, Genette's observation that every narrative is told by a narrator and that the narrator must be perceived as "itself fictive, even if assumed directly by the author" (213), has been widely adopted. Besides, the concept of omniscience or of an authorial narrative situation nowadays entails that the narrator is explicit but not a part of the story world. So, Friedman's "elimination" of the narrator can be contested, but, other than that, his "selective omniscience" can be used in a constructive way by stressing a very important and also correct observation he makes in his chapter on multiple selective omniscience: "Here the reader ostensibly listens to no one; the story comes directly through the minds of the characters" (127). This feature, as well as any other feature of multiple selective omniscience apart from the higher number of selected focal characters, is also applicable to selective omniscience (ibid.128). After all, it is true that by the use of selective omniscience, the reader gets the impression that the story unfolds through Mailer and, thus, concentrates on everything Mailer perceives and reflects on. As it will also unfold gradually in the course of this analysis, the decision to use this particular narrative situation for the larger part of *Armies* must be seen as one of the two important narratological components which add to the novel's specific form of new journalism.

The other important component consists in the abovementioned divergences. It is a very notable feature of *Armies* that the large sections of fixed internal focalization are interspersed with smaller sections that read like a nonfocalized narrative. In these sections, the reader is drawn away from the action and is explicitly approached by the narrator who otherwise 'hides' behind and almost 'masquerades' as Mailer. This in a way happens by framing the focalized parts of the narrative. Right at the beginning of the novel, the narrator explicitly approaches and even actively includes the narratee in his plans and actions saying: "From the outset let us bring you news of your protagonist" (3) and ends the chapter suggesting, "Now we may leave *Time* in order to find out what happened" (4). That way, he introduces Mailer as the protagonist and, thus, center of the narrative. After having inserted an article from *Time* magazine, he now takes the opportunity to announce to the narratee that he is from now on actively included in the narrator's task to dismiss seemingly 'objective' accounts of the event by letting Book One function as a more reliable source, a subjective 'inside scoop' of the march. Accordingly, the second chapter directly opens with Mitchell Goodman calling Norman Mailer and thus explains how Mailer became master of ceremony and one of the leaders of the demonstration. In line with that, the narrative situation switches to fixed internal focalization or selective omniscience, which becomes obvious when Mailer's thoughts about his aversion to conversations on the telephone are described in a number of paragraphs long before the reader even gets to know who is on the other end. Because of its focus on Mailer, this type of point of view is regarded as appropriate for a reliable description of the march.

A similar situation occurs at the beginning of part II of Book One, after part I has ended with Mailer speaking to the protesters at the Ambassador Theater in Washington. Here, the narrator first explains to the narratee why Mailer has qualified as protagonist, a decision to be discussed in chapter 3.3. He then continues to involve the narratee by talking of "our particular protagonist" and invites him to trace what happens saying "Let us follow further"(53-54). In keeping with Friedman's typology, the narrative situation of such sections can be identified as "editorial omniscience." Whereas the term selective omniscience implies that the narrator rather fades into the background, editorial omniscience indicates that the story is explicitly told by its 'editor', the author, who either speaks as "I," which does not happen in *Armies*, or "we," including the narratee, which happens frequently (cf. Friedman 121). In such 'framing' sections the author clearly governs his material, comments, and may even talk about something completely unrelated to the story (ibid.). Although some devices and passages of *Armies*, to be discussed below, give reason to believe that the narrator is identical to the real author of the text, for the sake of contemporary narratology it seems more sensible to indicate preliminary doubts about the presence of an "author-narrator" (Friedman 133), which is why "author" will be put in brackets in what follows. Eventually, to further specify the (author-)narrator's diegetic level, in such somewhat framing passages where the story comes to a stop he appears to be extradiegetic. In the 'frames' he indicates that he is also the one who is narrating in the passages of selective omniscience because he invites the narratee to join him. And in the focalized sections, where he seems to hide behind the protagonist Mailer, he is still not a part of the story world and is therefore a heterodiegetic narrator.

The (author-)narrator's addresses to the narratee and his revelation of the construction process of the narrative are particularly noticeable features of the passages where he becomes explicit. According to Genette, these two features signal important "extranarrative functions" of the narrator, namely the "function of communication" and the "directing function" (255-57). As for the former, the narrator frequently approaches a narratee who must necessarily be situated on the same diegetic level. Thus, the extradiegetic narrator approaches an extradiegetic narratee who is identical to the implied reader with whom, in turn, a real reader of the narrative can easily identify (Genette 260). The natural effect of the narrator's address to the narratee is the impression that the narrator considers his interlocutor to be at eye level with him. What is more, one can argue that this sense of equality is sometimes even taken to a level of privacy in *Armies* since the narrator also involves the narratee in the decisions he makes as a constructor of the narrative, assuring him "you are in on the secret" (17).

The quite distinctive directing function of the narrator finds expression in numerous comments on the organization of the narrative. This can, for example, take place by means of advance notices which are often put in brackets and thus marked as insertions within the actual plot. An example is the note "(Explanations about the position of Paul Goodman will follow later)" (19). Sometimes, such comments even read like proper 'stage directions' as in the narrator's announcement that "[t]he scene now shifts to Washington" (236). In order to point out possible effects of this directing function, the beginning of chapter one of part IV, Book One, provides a good section for analysis. After wide passages of selective omniscience in which the narrator describes how Mailer experiences the actual demonstration and how he is finally arrested for transgressing a police line, here, the reader suddenly finds himself confronted with a radical disruption and a narrator who explains why this disruption is actually taking place. This time, the (author-)narrator seems to refer to himself in the third person as "the Novelist" (133) – one of the decisive hints that suggest the possibility of a personal union of Norman Mailer as the real author of *Armies* and the narrator of Book One – but continues to include the reader by speaking of "our history" (ibid.). Well aware that the reader is eager to know what happens to Mailer after he is dragged off by the MPs, the narrator takes a minute to reflect on the rupture by which he wants "to deepen the addiction of his audience" (ibid.). He describes the delay and his appearance as "Victorian practice" which "modern audiences," he worries, will not accept but put away the book and turn on the TV instead (ibid.). Very ironically, he therefore explains that, in general, "a modern novelist must apologize, even apologize profusely, for daring to leave his narrative, he must in fact absolve himself of the charge of employing a device, he must plead necessity" (ibid.) and, seemingly referring to himself, finally apologizes: "So the Novelist now pleads necessity." (ibid.)

Interestingly enough, by laying bare and commenting on the organization of his narrative, the narrator reveals a lot about the nature of fiction or literature in general. The self-reflexivity of his narrating, in the former example the talk about why he tells the story the way he does, attests to "a metafictional awareness of its [i.e. literature's] own constructedness and textuality" (Huber et al. 8), which is also aroused in the reader due to its open display. Self-reflexivity naturally opens up the field of metafiction. Thus, in order to understand what effects the specific metafictional strategies applied in *Armies* have, one has to figure out what the concept of metafiction entails and what it works against.

Metafiction is generally referred to as "a kind of self-reflexive narrative that narrates about narrating" (Imhof 9). However, *Armies* is rather interspersed by passages in which the narrator actually refers to the construction process of the narrative or the application of older narrative conventions and is thus probably best described as containing parts of "self-conscious fiction" (ibid. 12) – a phrase which is reminiscent of the self-reflexivity involved. As the act of narrating becomes central in metafiction, everything that is linked to narrating such as the rules and techniques the narrator has to abide by and apply is turned into a major subject (ibid. 9). According to Rüdiger Imhof, this must be regarded as a response to an underlying conviction among 20th-century metafictionists that fiction is the only "knowable entity" (19). Still, although fiction became itself a subject of writing, the underlying theme and aim of this habit was an exploration of the relationship between literature and life (ibid. 9). Convinced that "reality is a subjective metal [sic!] phenomenon" (ibid. 27), the metafictionists drew the logical conclusion that "a narrative [...] cannot represent reality; it can only create a reality *sui generis*" (ibid. 10). Consequently, they did not put much effort in the creation of a reality effect as generated in realist fiction. On the contrary, they actually preferred to destroy such an effect by uncovering the creation/description paradox in fiction – a term used to designate that "[*d*]*escriptions* of objects in fiction are simultaneously *creations* of that object" (Waugh 88). In *Armies* this is not only achieved by the narrator's report on his aspirations, which instantly reminds the reader of the fact that what he is reading (although it did happen in reality) is made up, fictionalized, but also by allusions to the (alleged) novel/history dichotomy, which will be elaborated on in chapter 3.3. After his speech at the Ambassador, Mailer decides to join McDonald at a party of some liberal academics. Describing the rest of Mailer's night, the narrator remarks: "Of course if this were a novel, Mailer would spend the rest of the night with a lady. But it is history, and so the Novelist is for once blissfully removed from any description of the hump-your-backs of sex. Rather he can leave such matters to the happy or unhappy imagination of the reader." (52) The reader is left wondering whether Mailer did actually go home alone or not, but the important thing about this comment is that the narrator is mocking novelistic conventions. In a novel, he assures, the reader's desire for a love story-strand – or at least a titillating affair – would have been fulfilled, but what he is dealing with here is obviously not a novel in its purest sense.

It is clear by now that metafiction heavily depends on the commitment of a "self-conscious narrator" (Imhof 36). Obviously, he is giving the reader a very hard time settling into the narrative as he does his best to show that he does not care about what Patricia Waugh calls a "'commonsense' reality" (90). He could have decided to passively "order[] the chaos of experience and shape[] it into a comprehensible whole," as Mas'ud Zavarzadeh describes the aesthetic patterning of "the classic novel" (6), but points out instead how he actively constructs a narrative about real life matters. To work against the creation of a mere illusion of reality, he further mocks the rather passive reception of realist fiction since he explicitly asks the reader to assist him as an active "co-producer" (Imhof 253). As the novel contains many indications of a personal union of narrator and real author, it is moreover particularly interesting to note that in metafiction the self-conscious narrator "may be taken for the real author's mouthpiece" (ibid. 36). Accordingly, in his study on contemporary metafiction Imhof suggests the term "author-narrator" (ibid. 40) – the same term that Friedman uses to describe the voice in works told in editorial omniscience. Therefore, one could argue that the narrator does in fact speak of himself when he lets "the Novelist" apologize profusely for his disruptions. With regard to the last chapter of Book One, one could furthermore claim that the narrator reflects on his own experiences when he describes how the protagonist Mailer "contracted to write an account of the March on the Pentagon, and wrestled with the difficulties of how to do it" (215), since he also feels like he has to justify the way he tells his story due to the modern reader's alleged impatience. And even the narrator's demand "Let us then make our comic hero the *narrative vehicle* for the March on the Pentagon" (54, my italics), which actually announces that the protagonist Mailer functions as a personal medium, the abovementioned "central figure" of the event from whose point of view the story is told, would at second glance come to read like a latent indication that Mailer is also the narrator. This, in fact, would even make it a threefold appearance of Mailer as real author, narrator, and protagonist.

However, in the end, the real author Mailer's presence as narrator of *Armies* cannot be pointed out for certain. Instead of referring to himself in the third person, when speaking of "the Novelist" the narrator could after all just be talking about Norman Mailer, the real author, who does write his novel but lets a fictitious narrator apologize on his behalf. Furthermore, the analogy between the problems of the protagonist – who doubtlessly does correspond to Norman Mailer – and the narrator could as well be just coincidental. But, then again, it is probably precisely this constant oscillation between authorial appearance and disappearance in the respective narrative sections that constitutes what with reference to contemporary notions of the 'death of the author' may be called Mailer's very own 'return of the author.' As both writer and person he appears and/or seems to appear in so many ways that the narrator's comment, "He felt he had been part of a literary game" (21), which actually refers to Mailer's doubts about the sincerity of Robert Lowell's praise for Mailer's works, comes to read like a side-swipe at the complexity that Mailer's omnipresence entails.

Eventually, Mailer's particular 'return of the author' instantly goes along with what Brian McHale calls "the postmodernist *topos* of the writer at his desk" (198). By means of metafiction and self-reflexivity, he makes sure the reality of his writing situation is pointed out in the narrative so that the reader in turn becomes aware of the reality of his reading situation. As soon as this has happened, McHale argues, the author is automatically introduced into the fiction and even included so-to-speak as a fictional character in the mind of the reader (197-98). In *Armies*, this notion is even realized in that Mailer becomes a *real* character, the protagonist.

To sum up, *Armies* probably constitutes the most interesting and intricate manifestation of Mailer's habit to let his own personality inform his narrators and protagonists. The protagonist is named Mailer and is clearly the real author's *alter ego*. The narrator in turn provides the reader with numerous indications of being the real author's other *alter ego* but leaves the reader speculating. However, it turns out that in terms of the narrative technique, it is exactly this play with authorial presence and absence that chiefly contributes to this novel's specific form of new journalism. The intertwining of two narrative perspectives, selective and editorial omniscience, provides the basis for this 'hide-and-seek,' and, equally important, offers a solution to the difficult question of how to depict the relationship between Mailer and the event he experiences. In passages of selective omniscience, an illusory separation between Mailer and the march, as would have been created in realist fiction and conventional journalism, is avoided. As the focus is on the protagonist and as the event virtually passes through him, the reader gains insight into Mailer's personal interpretation of the event. But still, the fact that these passages of Book One are told in the third person and therefore read like a report nonetheless adds a certain distance, which is probably due to Mailer's endeavor to strike a balance between 'historical' meaning journalistic account and novel. Like in human interest reporting, which requires the reporter to hold a certain distance to the person he writes on, Mailer must keep his distance to himself. Quite contrarily, in passages of editorial omniscience, the narrator's explicit metafictional reader-addresses and his self-reflexive comments on the fiction-making process prevent the reader from indulging into the story world. Instead, they clearly point to the fictionalized nature of the narrative and evoke a feeling of privacy between narrator and reader. *Armies* is insofar very much informed by a postmodern radical break with an illusory mimetic aesthetic in the spirit of realist fiction, mentioned in chapter 2.1.3. As, according to Ansgar Nünning, an "increasing degree of self-reflexivity [...] is characteristic of postmodern novels in general and fictional biographies and autobiographies in particular" (196), the new journalism in *Armies* appears to be very much in line with a general trend in postmodern writing. Mailer manages to publish a significant event in his life in book form and does not only fictionalize but 'metafictionalizes' it. In doing so, he, the real author, does not only function as "the vehicle of autobiographical *fact* within the projected fictional world; and as the *maker* of that world" (McHale 202), but also as protagonist and maybe even narrator. In line with a postmodern "playful spirit" that informs metafiction (Imhof 18) and the observation that "[p]ostmodernist fiction has brought the author back to the surface" (ibid. 199), Mailer lets himself appear in more or less transparent ways. His new journalistic return of the author is therefore an intentionally puzzling, postmodern act.

3.2 "Like most cloudy metaphors, this served to get him home" – Style and Figurative Language

During the demonstration, Mailer comes to reflect on various issues of American culture, society, and politics. His thoughts thereby range from meditative associational streams ("Then his thoughts began to meander again" (*Armies* 158)) over "rumination[s]" (ibid. 154) to active contemplation, sheer brooding, and thus take on various forms of individual sensemaking. Mailer's mind is constantly busy absorbing what is happening around him in order to discover the meaning of this particular event in contemporary American history. From time to time, however, his imagination is so vivid that the (author-)narrator drops remarks which mock Mailer's thinking. For example, before he goes on stage in the Ambassador Theater, he has to use the bathroom but misses the bowl, which causes him to imagine the most absurd consequences would the mess he leaves behind be discovered. This imaginary episode is subsequently ridiculed by the comment "(Out of such stuff is a novelist's brain)" (31).

The constant associating is significantly reflected in the style. When Mailer is ruminating, the sentences tend to be long and complex. They could almost be described as written in the spirit of a Joycean stream of consciousness. Due to their numerous dashes and parantheses they surely work against readability, but they mirror an active mind. Apart from the sentence structure, the word-choice is also quite complex. On the one hand, in passages of direct speech it sometimes seems that swear words are everything Mailer, the rhetorician, needs to express himself. In his speech to the demonstrators, for example, he chooses a rather explicit rhetoric crying out "'We're going to try to stick it up the government's ass'" (38) and counts on "sh*t's metaphorical associations" (ibid.) when he goes on "'I'm as full of shit as Lyndon Johnson'" (49). On the other hand, Mailer's thoughts are for the most part characterized by sophisticated, weighty words which reflect a serious examination of the issues he comes to think about. The words appear to be chosen carefully and in combination with the lengthy sentences therefore encourage equally careful reading.

In line with the multitude of associational streams which permeate the whole novel, the language is equally rich in figures of speech. As it is Mailer's goal to arrive at an interpretation of the march, a powerful figurative language seems to suggest itself. Like the intricate sentence structure and the distinctive diction, the figures one encounters are also fairly unconventional. As might be anticipated by his personification of the novel as 'bitch goddess,' Mailer draws a lot of unusual comparisons which most of the time require additional explanation. A *tertium comparationis* can often not be discovered or otherwise only be guessed which hinders the figurative process. Luckily, as will be pointed out, in his unstoppable search for meaning, Mailer does some of the explaining himself. Potential figures virtually just open up to Mailer as the march and the events surrounding it proceed. As the protagonist experiences the most bizarre reality, objects which, one might think, deny any comparison or interpretation whatsoever, constitute the richest carriers of personal experience. More often than not, the figures are thereby not just punctually incorporated in the narrative but take up a lot of space and become essential components. Nearly every page piles figure upon figure, so in what follows, only the most recurrent and distinct, and therefore most representative ones can be discussed.

To begin with, as in previous works, Mailer's aversion to the advancing permeation of technology in American society is also emphasized in *Armies*. "Technology" and "technological" are given a metaphorical meaning and ultimately become highly loaded key words in Mailer's vocabulary, signaling threat and America's gradual decay. Mailer is, for example, living in "technology land" (e.g. 15, 92), one of his favorite metaphors to depict the U.S. At the beginning of Book One it is suggested what life in technology land entails. Before the night at the Ambassador, Mailer attends a party of a young liberal couple. Entering their home, the interior design instantly causes in him a feeling of deep depression. With its "functional" furniture, the "institutional brown and library gray" colors and "abstract" paintings and sculptures, the apartment smells like "the scent of the void which comes off the pages of a

Xerox copy" (15). In line with the technologically produced void, Mailer regards host and hostess as "liberal technologues" who have "no root of a real war with technology land itself," but are "the natural managers of that future air-conditioned vault where the last of human life would still exist" (15-16). They are ultimately mere "servants of that social machine of the future" (16) that destroys nature, convinced that they have the upper-hand and unaware of the dominance of technology. Further comparisons and descriptions which signal the omnipresence of technology are numerous. Lowell looks at Mailer with a "light winging off like a mad laser from his eye" (20) and on Friday morning, Mailer wakes up having a "thunderous electronic headache" (54-55) which foreshadows his fight against a "technological century" (54) about to start at night. When the sit-in starts after the end of the demonstration, the marshals begin to arrest people at random. At first sight, these arrests seem to be meaningless. However, for Mailer they attest to "the deepest sort of technological meaning" (271); their purpose is to avoid that the arrested feel like martyrs. Since they are chosen randomly, they may feel like victims or fools, but this kind of arrest does not evoke a feeling of pride. Because of that "technical wisdom" of the marshals, the arrests are eventually "more brutal" than any justifiable detention (ibid).

As one can see, 'technology' is a metaphor that comes to stand for a lot of different but always negative things. With regard to the passages just mentioned, the tenors to that uniquely Mailerian vehicle are void, artificiality, destruction, oppression, and brutality. But what is it about *literal* technology that causes Mailer to adopt it as one of his most recurrent metaphors? According to Mailer, the increasing modernization of every area of life has already caused "alienation" of the American population (154). A decisive technological invention that is chiefly to blame for this is the TV. In chapter 3.1 it has been mentioned that in one of the metafictional digressions the (author-)narrator pretends to apologize profoundly for the delay he causes since he knows his modern audience is at all times tempted to put away the book and switch on the TV. In the course of the novel, however, it becomes clear that this is not really a joking matter. When Mailer joins other protesters who have been arrested in a bus which is about to bring them to Occoquan, he notices that they look remarkably like stereotyped high school kids he knows from TV series. As a result, he comes to think about the influence of TV on American society. TV, he knows, "direct[s] the styles and the manners and therefore the ideas of America" which are "ideas like conformity, cleanliness, America-is-always-right" (156). Mailer even wrote an essay about his observation that no American novelist ever accomplished to write a major novel that would appeal to the bigger part of "that American audience brainwashed by Hollywood, TV, and *Time*" (157).[9] And in a speech to the Modern Language Association he once argued that because American realist literature failed to make people aware of their own identity, in the 20th century movies, the mass media, and the TV at home fill that void with a "meretricious, commercial art that disproportionately shapes the consciousness of the people" (Begiebing 4). This eventually causes them to lose some of their deepest human experiences which are "unconscious, spiritual, telepathic, and primitive" (ibid. 2, 4). So in the end, it turns out that there is a much more serious tone to the (author-)narrator's apology than one might assume.

In line with the description of the liberal couple as "technologues," there is also a specific Mailerian language that goes along with that term, namely "technologese" (*Armies* 284). It is a language "which succeeds in stripping itself of any moral content," and is therefore the only way of expression for people like the Pentagon spokesman who defends himself against charges of violence by demonstrators using scientific law code-like jargon (ibid.). In Mailer's vocabulary, technologese is further synonymous with "totalitarianese" (ibid.). Totalitarianism is another abstract metaphor by which Mailer, in Robert J. Begiebing's words, "refers generally to that tendency in the modern world to regiment and pacify life, to homogenize diversity and individuality, and to stifle dissent and change" (3). Mailer uses totalitarianism interchangeably with "cancer" because he considers it to be "the disease of our time" (ibid.) and aims to underline the destructive force inherent in today's power struggles. For years, Mailer had been striving for an exploration of the nature of totalitarianism. According to him, the main goal of totalitarianism is "to render populations apathetic," which is achieved by "the destruction of mood" (*Armies* 117).

At this point, it is interesting to note that Mailer's thoughts on the disposition of technology and totalitarianism almost read like the scholarly views on mass and counter culture of the 1960s sketched before. The idea of the TV as a director of American values such as conformity, for example, corresponds to the image of the TV as domestic equivalent to containment policy. Moreover, Mailer's understanding of totalitarianism as a subversive homogenizing force is reminiscent of mass culture's homogenization of difference as attested by Huyssen. And Roszak's concept of a technocracy, a regime of experts that exploits people's dependency on technological objects and unfolds as subliminal and oppressive as totalitarianism, comes very close to the connotations of Mailer's key metaphors technology and totalitarianism.

---

[9] It will be elaborated on the criticism of the press expressed in *Armies* in more detail in chapter 3.3.

While technology and totalitarianism constitute highly loaded terms that Mailer had already embraced as two of his most distinct metaphors before he wrote *Armies*, some other figures are rather unique to the novel for they are objects and places Mailer encounters as the march advances or contemporary events and concepts to which Mailer's attention is drawn. A significant example of an object that turns into a recurrent figure is the Pentagon. When the march begins, the protesters are only able to catch a far-away glimpse of the building, but for most of the time the Pentagon is completely out of sight. Although still far away from the goal, Mailer already senses its figurative power. It is "the symbol, the embodiment, [...] the true and high church of the military-industrial complex," so he immediately grasps its totalitarian function personifying it as the "blind five-sided eye of a subtle oppression which had come to America" (113). As these associations lead him to a furious portrayal of the destructive nature of the 20th century, the tenors of the Pentagon metaphor become more radical as well. The "high church" of America is at the same time the "anus of corporation land, [...] destroying the future of its own nation with each day it augment[s] in strength" (114). However, when the marchers finally reach their goal, the Pentagon is hardly visible, so Mailer has to recollect the first time he saw it. It had actually not looked more impressive than on pictures. Nonetheless, its appearance had a powerful effect on Mailer as the following quote shows:

> The Pentagon rose like an anomaly of the sea from the soft Virginia fields (they were crossing a park), its pale yellow walls reminiscent of some plastic plug coming out of the hole made in flesh by an unmentionable operation. There, it sat, geometrical aura complete, isolated from anything in nature surrounding it. (116)

The simile "like an anomaly of the sea" clearly suggests that this government building contrasts sharply with the nature surrounding it. Although Mailer is merely crossing a park, in the face of the unnatural apparition before him, the lawn suddenly seems like vast fields. Positioned like an architectonical embodiment of mass culture, the "plastic plug" is obviously misplaced and the fact that it "mak[es] nature look like an outdoor hospital" (117) leads Mailer to ruminate about oppressive strategies of totalitarianism. Since the stifling quality of totalitarianism destroys mood, a "scent which r[ises] from the acts and calms of nature, [...] totalitarianism [is] a deodorant to nature" (ibid.). As a result, Mailer expands the figurative meaning of the Pentagon: "Yes, and by the logic of this metaphor, the Pentagon looked like the five-sided tip on the spout of a spray can" (ibid.).

Along with the authoritative, pessimistic connotations of the Pentagon, other places and issues related to the march are also given symbolic meaning. Washington is, for instance, frequently referred to as the "capital of technology land" (e.g. 93) and Mailer regards the war in Vietnam as "Uncle Sam's Whorehouse War" and "the progressive contamination of all American life" (97, 51). However, Mailer does not only blame the government for the involvement in Vietnam. For him, the war is only a symptom of "the secret hope of a bigger war" that might eventually free the nation of the suffocating impact of technology (154). He therefore identifies the American small town as the "true war party of America" (ibid.). It supports violent acts as it is itself searching for "insanity," a sense of living that has been wiped out by technology (153).

Recapitulating the most striking features of Mailer's style and figurative language, it is very noticeable that the style at all times reflects the situation Mailer is in. When he is acting as MC, his speech is shaped by swear words that are indicative of his desire to move the crowd and make his co-marchers aware of the importance of the event. He regards the demonstration as an "existential situation" (38) and must therefore act like an "existential philosopher" (134), like the hipster he himself defined in the 1950s. Caught up in society but still examining it from a certain distance, it is his task to explore the very nature of the situation he is in. While the "champion of obscenity" (134) in him is exposed as he enters the stage yelling at the crowd in order to compensate for the diffidence of his fellow-speakers, he learns more about the event's disposition when he contemplates. As his thoughts unfold freely, the sentences get more complex in accordance. While this does not serve the ends of easy readability, it is a largely unadulterated eye-witness report and therefore authentic. It has been stated above that for Mailer, finding an appropriate style is not only a matter of aesthetics but itself a way of self-exploration. In the novel it says that "the truth of his material was revealed to a good writer by the cutting edge of his style" (87-88), so the way Mailer's observations, thoughts, and associations are reflected in his style, ultimately traces Mailer's path to his personal truth.

Clearly, this path is hardly illuminated by reason. Instead, Mailer's rich figurative language is indicative of a faith in the power of imagination. Thomas McLaughlin argues that figures always appeal to the irrational and to man's deep desire to arrive at a "self-evident truth" (88). The truth that unfolds through Mailer's figures is thus very dark and pessimistic, which results in a general tone of the novel being equally dismal and threatening. Besides, his figures are "'spectacular' figures," figures that are visibly figurative (ibid. 90). Mailer's metaphors are prominent because the vehicles are contemporary things and objects that come to stand for contemporary menaces to American society. He is constantly torn between reality and fantasy, absorbing everything around him and turning it into epic metaphors, which by their obvious uniqueness avoid the illusion that a fixed meaning is present in the world and, like the choice of a selective omniscience-point of view, emphasize that they are expressions of a very personal act of sense-making. As an equivalent to the self-reflexivity in Mailer's narrative technique, his specific figurative language is a "natural expression of his epistemology since it openly displays meaning as an individual consciousness's active projection of its [...] interpretive abilities upon the world around it, abilities in which he has a romantic's confidence" (Hellmann 42). It this struggle "between romanticism and rationalism, between the recklessly existential individual and the relentlessly manipulated mass" (Guttmann 103) that works against destructive forces in society. Forces such as technology "destroy the deepest experiences of mankind, which originate in metaphor" (Begiebing 2) so that it becomes Mailer's strategy to reinstate metaphor by giving them a metaphorical meaning. This is an easy task because for him these forces practically lend themselves to metaphor. Mailer thus once more fictionalizes reality. The outcome can be described as 'factional metaphors;' metaphors whose vehicles are taken from reality, whereas the tenors are bizarre, obscene and threatening, producing an image of an increasingly fictional life. The epistemological concern with the relationship of symbolic frameworks to what they represent, according to David Eason an increasingly important issue in new journalism (142), is performed by Mailer. He does not only elicit meaning himself, but also reflects on this active sense-making process: "Like most cloudy metaphors, this served to get him home – there is nothing like the search for a clear figure of speech to induce gyroscopic intensity sufficient for the compass to work." (82) Begiebing argues that "[t]he new journalism [...] becomes for Mailer a vehicle for discovering as well as for portraying [...] the mythic and symbolic in the literal" (164) and he is surely right. However, as could be seen, when Mailer tries to make sense of what he sees, his interpretations are oftentimes as 'enigmatic' as the reality before his eyes. He is able "to bridge self and event through [...] metaphor" (Hellmann 37) but his long and abstract interpretations are often themselves so figurative that they could be described as "meta-interpretation[s]," a term Mas'ud Zavarzadeh uses to show that they "turn[] into an anti-interpretation; a negation of the proposed reading of reality" (155). In the end, meaning is elicited but in a way that seems to suggest that reality can ultimately not be interpreted in a rational manner.

3.3 "History as a Novel, the Novel as History" – The Interrelation between Form and Contents

It is interesting to see that many structural elements of the novel reflect its contents. Mailer's experience of the march as well as the new journalistic overall theme to arrive at a larger truth of the event provides the structural framework of *Armies*. The exploration of the interrelation between form and content of the novel will constitute the last step in its analysis. This aspect is examined last because it provides a broader overview of Mailer's intentions and the success or failure of his way to strike a balance between novel and report. Moreover, the analyses of the previous two chapters provide a basis on which the following analysis must draw and build since it explores the sense-making process as expressed in the 'bigger whole,' the structure. The following components are of particular interest for an examination of the relation between form and content: The novel's division into Book One and Book Two, Book One's additional division into four parts, the title, the subtitle, and certain chapter titles.

Mailer's main goal to arrive at an interpretation of reality is already suggested in the subtitle "History as a Novel, the Novel as History." The subtitle moreover indicates Mailer's concern with form and anticipates the division of the novel into Book One and Book Two. The first and much larger part "Book One" is entitled "History as a Novel: The Steps of the Pentagon" and comprises the article "The Steps of the Pentagon" which Mailer wrote for *Harper's Magazine*. In this part, the focus is on Mailer and his personal perception of the peace march. The second part is entitled "The Novel as History: The Battle of the Pentagon" and contains the follow-up article "The Battle of the Pentagon," published in *Commentary* only one month later. Although it initially deals with the problems David Dellinger, chairman of the "National Mobilization to End the War in Vietnam" and designer of the march, has to face, the second part focuses on no particular character and contains a lot of background information about the event. Hellmann argues that in new journalism aesthetic form "ultimately determines the selection and presentation of facts" (25). In this respect, *Armies* can be seen as a prime example for a work whose content is shaped by its structure. In order to elaborate on this assertion, the most prominent structural element, the division into Book One and Book Two, will be examined at first so that its impact on its subdivisions and its contents can be explained.

The title of Book One, "History as a Novel: The Steps of the Pentagon," indicates that Mailer's real-life experiences during the peace march are conveyed in a novelistic manner. And indeed, in what follows, the focus on the protagonist Mailer and the highly metaphorical language contribute chiefly to the impression that one is reading a novel. The fictionalization of the occurrences in Washington works so smoothly that the metafictional, self-reflexive remarks of the (author-)narrator, by which he points to the making of the novel, might even seem a little over the top. However, taking the very beginning of *Armies* into consideration, they can be regarded as serving a distinct purpose. Book One opens with an article from *Time* magazine which deals with the period from Mailer's speech at the Ambassador until his arrest. It christens Mailer the "anti-star" of the march and basically makes him look like a wretched drunkard whose only argument is a well-placed "fuck you" (3-4). Right after the article has finished, the (author-)narrator steps in declaring "Now we may leave *Time* in order to find out what happened" (4). Through his appearance as a narrator he clearly points out the novelistic nature of book one but also indicates that he is going to tell the truth about something that happened in real life. In accordance, what follows is a perfectly stereotyped beginning of a novel, though a novel about real life: "On a day somewhat early in September, the year of the first March on the Pentagon, 1967, the phone rang one morning and Norman Mailer, operating on his own principle of war games and random play, picked it up." (4) Mailer could not distance himself more clearly from the press, and also from writing a report. Still, he cannot help but show that he also does not take himself too seriously by mocking his constant preoccupation with war and mischief. In accordance, Book One sets itself apart from the article through its narrative technique and also through its style and its figurative language. While the article contains easy tag phrases which serve the ends of easy readability, the sentence structure of Book One and the highly metaphorical language are very complex. Given these distinct differences, it almost seems as though Mailer and the narrator want to underline Cyril Connolly's statement cited in the introduction, but not without stressing that journalism does not necessarily have to be true even though it is easily 'grasped at once.' Besides, criticism of the press is also expressed in more explicit ways as the novel is interspersed with disparaging remarks. It has been said before that the (author-)narrator regards *Time* as a brainwashing entity. However, this magazine comes to stand for America's whole media landscape. The media brainwash through constant misrepresentation and Mailer is even personally affected. He is deeply concerned because he knows about the media's powerful impact on their and hence also his audience: "So a particular sadness slipped sooner or later into every good writer – they were kept further removed from uneducated readers by the general horrors of journalistic mistranscription than by the difficulty of their work." (65)

The initial impulse is therefore to arrive at a novel about history. Paradoxically, despite the aforementioned novelistic features, the impression that one is reading a novel is disturbed by the subdivision of Book One into part I – IV. The four parts structure Mailer's experiences from Goodman's phone call until his release after the arrest and are entitled "Thursday Evening," "Friday Afternoon," "Saturday Matinée," and "Saturday Night and All of Sunday." Information about day and time of the respective occurrences indicates an overall structure in the spirit of journalistic reporting and is probably due to the original structure of Mailer's article which underlies Book One. The fact that Book One therefore rather comes to read like a 'novelistic article' foreshadows that the title "History *as* a Novel" (my italics) should not be interpreted as announcing a pure novel about history but rather a history that 'masquerades' as a novel. The fictionalization of the event has served the purpose to underline Mailer's personal view on the event, but its real-life origin is still shining through.

Generally speaking, Book Two can be regarded as the counterpart of Book One. Entitled "The Novel as History," it tries to uncover the backgrounds of the event which seem so fictional, so 'novelistic' to Mailer, and it also tries to appear as a historical, meaning journalistic, account. In an attempt to show that there is yet another side to the march, it largely refrains from fictionalizing techniques. Like a regular journalistic article, it is written in the third person and does not focus on any character in specific. In contrast to the misrepresentative accounts Mailer has had to cope with so far, Book Two tries to work against misreporting in that it heavily relies on facts and figures and discusses numerous articles taken from the most diverse newspapers. It turns out that none of the inserted articles, be they from renowned papers like the *New York Times*, independent papers like the Washington *Free Press*, or underground papers like the *Mobilizer*, paint an adequate picture of the demonstration. The narrator concludes that the press is "naturally on the side of the authority" and the underground press is "sure to distort [...] the real history of the events to [its] own need" (266). The attempt of Book Two to arrive at an objective 'report' finally fails as well. In accordance with the (author-)narrator of Book One who exposes the fictionalization of the first part of *Armies*, the fact that Book Two is simply crammed with detailed background information and articles about the march destroys the illusion of a truly objective account of the event. It seems rather like an artificial objectification, and is therefore reminiscent of practices such as those of the Associated Press that rendered its news objective in order to appeal to its clientele. Besides, the (author-)narrator also appears in Book Two – though by far not as frequently as in Book One – and guides the reader through the text. His appearance does the same with Book Two that the informational headings of the four parts do with Book One. It has the effect that the fictional nature of the march is shining through and therefore gives the impression that what one is reading is still Mailer's thoughts, even though he is not explicitly named or instated as protagonist.

Obviously, neither of the two parts is exclusively historical or novelistic; both disclose features of either style. But why is it that Mailer obviously decided to be the 'imperfect' novelist and journalist so many critics see in him? The reasons lie in Mailer's skeptical attitude towards the march. He does not necessarily approve of it but participates in it with all his energy. For him, it is an "idiot mass manifestation[] which could only drench one in the most ineradicable kind of mucked-up publicity and have for compensation nothing" (18). When he first hears of it, he is convinced of "the redundancy of these projects" and asks himself, "When was everyone going to cut out the nonsense and get to work, do their own real work? One's own literary work was the only answer to the war in Vietnam" (9). Yet when the march is about to start he draws a lot of energy from the motivation of the young protesters. They are overcome by a "happy confidence that politics had again become mysterious, had begun to partake of Mystery; that gave life to a thought the gods were back in human affairs" (86). As one can see, on that weekend, two personalities constantly clash inside Mailer, that of the novelist and that of the activist. The one is convinced of the unique power of literature to reinstate the unconscious, mystic, and intuitive, the other believes in counter cultural protest as a way to free one's mind from technocracy and oppression. These two personalities are united in a novel about protest; an equally hybrid book on the borderline between literature and journalism.

Interestingly enough, this also explains why Mailer instates himself as protagonist. It is not only because he feels he must model his main character on himself in order to write a good book. This time, he explicitly needs his protagonist to set himself apart from what Radford calls "the Hearn-McLeod-Eitel group of doomed, liberal heroes; these characters, presented as men of considerable intelligence who are 'flawed' by their professionalism or their lack of 'courage', and defeated by the world in which they live" (41). Mailer is obviously different from his earlier heroes – and he presents himself as such. He is not too professional to become his own hero, and he is also not a coward. Since the novel aims at "recaptur[ing] the precise feel of the ambiguity of the event and its monumental disproportions" (53), Mailer is the perfect protagonist because he is "a figure of monumental disproportions and so serves willy-nilly as the bridge – many will say the *pons asinorum* – into the crazy house [...] of that historic moment" (53-54).

His 'disproportional' personality is revealed in two ways. On the one hand, he is referred to or thinks of himself variably. When Robert

Lowell calls him "the best journalist in America," Mailer almost feels insulted and tells Lowell "Well Cal, [...] there are days when I think of myself as being the best writer in America" (22). However, during the weekend in Washington, he develops some doubts about his writing skills and mocks himself constantly. In Washington he is only a "semi-distinguished and semi-notorious author" (15) and also an imperfect journalist, a "poor man's Papa" (200) – an allusion to his idol Ernest Hemingway. He moreover behaves like a "[r]evolutionar[y]-for-a-weekend" (56) and feels like a "vaudeville clown" (43). He does not take himself so seriously and thus becomes the "comic hero" (53) of the novel. One logical effect of that labeling is that the reader is increasingly assured that he is reading a very personal account. Drawing upon Enid Welsford's social and literary history of the fool, Robert J. Begiebing elaborates on other advantages of a comic hero. The comic relief that Mailer introduces into the novel by means of his actions and many humorous remarks indicates that "his wisdom is not of the intellect, but of the spirit" (146). "When he succeeds," Begiebing adds, the 'hero-fool' "represents the human emancipation from the stifling law or order [...] and its representatives who threaten to swallow the individual's original personality and freedom" (ibid.). This goes in line with Mailer's emphasis on intuition and his desire to work against the oppressive tendencies in contemporary America. On the other hand, a connection between Mailer's ambiguous personality and the ambiguous nature of the event is established by means of different epithets, which Mailer and the narrator use for Mailer in Book One, in order to point to the different functions he has to fulfill during and after the event. Being "witness and actor" (133) and "protagonist" (3) simultaneously requires an existence as "the Participant" (e.g. 12, 96) and "the Ruminant" (96) who take part in and reflect on the event. The epithets that prevail are, however, "the n/Novelist" (e.g. 11, 141, 55, 125) and "the Historian" (e.g. 13, 99).[10] Besides the impression evoked by the combination of informational headings and fictionalized content or by the appearance of the (author-)narrator in the more report-like Book Two, the personal union of Mailer as novelist and historian additionally contributes to the notion of a history 'masquerading' as a novel.

It has already been mentioned in chapter 3.1 that the issue of the novel/history dichotomy is even broached within the narrative. From time to time, the narrator puzzles the reader with comments on the novel's dual nature. However, some remarks also come to illuminate the

---

[10] Mailer's critical attitude towards the press may explain why the term "historian" is used instead of "journalist." As the narrator's or the real author's self-image as a 'historiographer of contemporary events' can be equated with that of a journalist, the terms "journalist" and "journalistic" will, for the sake of new journalism, also be used to describe the narrator's or Mailer's endeavor.

relation between structure and content. For instance, at the beginning of part II, the narrator explains why he chose Mailer to be the protagonist of an "intimate history" (53) of the march. And at the end of Book One, the whole novel is described as "his history of the Pentagon" which "insisted on becoming a history of himself over four days and therefore turned out to be "history in the costume of a novel" (215). In writing this 'masquerading' history Mailer is "delivered a discovery of what the March on the Pentagon [...] finally mean[s] [...] and so f[inds] himself ready at last to write a most concise Short History [...] which [...] will seek as History [...] to elucidate the mysterious character of that quintessentially American event" (216). As writing Book One has enabled him to grasp the meaning of the march which he considers to be the "first major battle of a war which may go on for twenty years" (88) – a war against dark forces in which he participates – he now feels ready to turn this novel into a history, into Book Two that "illustrates the darker passage and greater change for others" (Begiebing 157). The first chapter of Book Two explains how this is going to work in that it describes the "secret collaboration" (219) between novelist and historian. The novel must be regarded as a tower the novelist erects in the "forest of inaccuracy" created by the mass media (ibid.). The historian can now profit from it, stand on it, and study the event from a fresh angle. With regard to the interaction between structure and content, it is interesting to see that this chapter is entitled "A Novel Metaphor." It opens the history but instead of reporting, its title already points outward to the structure and stresses the metaphorical meaning of the novel that precedes. Five 'objectified' chapters later, the narrator declares that "the conceit one is writing a history must be relinquished" (254). The title of this chapter, "A Palette of Tactics," is again very telling as it indicates that the strategies are laid bare which have caused the dichotomy of the novel. The narrator explains that both books must be considered as hybrid; the novel because it is "to the best of the author's memory scrupulous to facts," and the history because it "is finally now to be disclosed as some sort of condensation of a collective novel" (255). However, in the end, the novel turns out to be the most appropriate genre because

> the difficulty is that the history is interior – no documents can give sufficient intimation: the novel must replace history at precisely that point where experience is sufficiently emotional, spiritual, psychical, moral, existential, or supernatural to expose the fact that the historian in pursuing the experience would be obliged to quit the clearly demarcated limits of historic inquiry (ibid.).

The very last chapter "The Metaphor Delivered" thus celebrates the novel's success. It is not said explicitly to which metaphor the title refers, but it is very likely that it is an allusion to the novel which has proven to stand for the best path to a personal truth. For Mailer, the march has shown that America has arrived at a point where it will either come to, as it is said, "give birth" to "the most fearsome totalitarianism the world has even known" or "a babe of a new world brave and tender" (288). However, through active resistance, people can still try to free themselves from the forces that keep them locked up. As Armin Paul Frank convincingly argues, the last chapter is an epilogue that finally leads one back into Mailer's thoughts (98). It is thus Mailer who is calling to the Americans: "Rush to the locks. Deliver us from our curse. For we must end on the road to that mystery where courage, death, and the dream of love give promise of sleep." (288)

In sum, the structural elements of *Armies* shed light on Mailer's intentions and so the content of the novel. In his illuminating study *Form as Content and Rhetoric in the Modern Novel* Michael Boccia bases his analyses on the observation that it is a "commonly held belief among modern writers" that "[n]arrative structure is both a metaphor of the themes and a form of rhetoric" (1). This can also be said of the postmodern Norman Mailer. Book One and Book Two are clearly shaped by Mailer's original intention to write a novel *and* a history of the peace march. But the hybrid nature of both parts eventually leads one to read the subtitle of the novel as pointing to the exchangeability of both parts. A clear-cut dichotomy can not be created but, as the metaphorical reference to the protesters as "armies" in the title already suggests, the novel, though impure, can ultimately best capture the factional feel of the event. The outcome is an account to which David Eason would refer as "metajournalism," a term he coined to indicate that in new journalism, in contrast to traditional journalism, "the form itself is part of the subject of the report" (qtd. in Schudson a, 187).

4 A (Re-)Construction of Truth – Truman Capote's *In Cold Blood: A True Account of a Multiple Murder and Its Consequences*

Truman Capote gloriously shot to fame when *In Cold Blood*, the first (so christened) 'non-fiction novel,' was published in 1965. Before, he had predominantly been concerned with writing fiction. Already his first published short story entitled "Miriam" (1942) received an O'Henry Award for Best First-Published Story, and his first novel *Other Voices, Other Rooms* (1948) stayed on the bestseller list of the *New York Times* for longer than two months. Working as a copy boy for the *New Yorker* magazine, his first new journalistic, or, for that matter, nonfiction piece was published in 1956 entitled "The Muses are Heard." It recorded a trip of the Everyman Opera to the Soviet Union and Capote went along all the way to write a witty, detailed, and often humorous account highlighting touchy subjects such as culture clash and communism.

Like "The Muses are Heard," and in line with Mailer's *Armies* having first been published in *Esquire*, his biggest success, *In Cold Blood*, was serialized in *The New Yorker* nine years later. Inspired by a small article, which he had read in *The New York Times* in 1959 and strongly supported by his editor, William Shawn, Capote decided to head to Kansas and investigate the quadruple murder. He felt he had chosen the perfect subject-matter because, as he told Harry Gilroy from *The New York Times*, "the human heart, being what it is, murder was a theme not likely to darken and yellow with time" (qtd. in Nuttall 132). At first, he planned to write a fairly extensive article, but after the two murderers had been arrested, he changed his mind and decided to create the first 'non-fiction novel.' In a frequently cited 1966 interview with George Plimpton from *The New York Times* he defined this allegedly new genre as "a narrative form that employed all the techniques of fictional art, but was nevertheless *immaculately factual*" (qtd. in ibid., my italics). It is easy to imagine that this objectivity claim created a big stir among fiction writers and journalists alike, and it is hardly surprising that skeptical views prevailed. In the Plimpton interview, Capote summed up the most frequent reproaches as follows: "They felt that what I proposed [...] was little more than a literary solution for fatigued novelists suffering from 'failure of the imagination'" (qtd. in ibid.). Nevertheless, the fact that the overwhelming response to the serial was even topped by the number of books being sold proved what Tom Wolfe observed as follows: "People of all sorts read *In Cold Blood*, people at every level of taste. Everybody was absorbed in it." (40-41) But Wolfe was also one of the first to point out that Capote had certainly not invented the genre he labeled the nonfiction novel. Instead, Wolfe claims that all Capote did was "to give his work the cachet of the reigning literary genre of his time, so that literary people would take it seriously" (52). However, one must also consider that Wolfe's "reigning literary genre" had by then not yet been named and described. Nick Nuttall defends Capote's innovative aspirations stating that "there was no 'cultural consensus' he could call on and, therefore, no pre-existing criteria to guide him in relation to form, style or subject matter" (132). So, although he definitely did not establish an entirely new genre, Capote was at least the first author to name and 'promote' one of the predominant literary genres of the 1960s soon to be called the new journalism or the nonfiction novel respectively. And he sure promoted it well. In a series of interviews he emphasized the truth claim he made in writing *In Cold Blood* and the novel's lead in the literary landscape of the late 1960s. After all, he was a novelist of long standing and not many dared to doubt his integrity. On the contrary, many journalists and some writers even came to follow suit. Capote's extraordinarily thorough research had inspired them in particular. Knowing that it had taken the author almost six years to write the novel – years in which he reconstructed the events that had taken place before he arrived in Kansas, interviewed the two killers, family members of the victims and the killers, and other people involved, and gathered information about the different settings – they felt they could report on virtually every subject as long as they got the inside scoop. As a consequence, they gained access to private parties and functions or even jeopardized their lives like, for example, John Sack who joined an infantry company to fight in Vietnam, which his nonfiction novel *M* (1967) is about. After the publication of *In Cold Blood* in 1965, the new journalism, though yet unnamed, fully sprang to life and began to arouse public interest; Capote had finally become the trend-setter he had always claimed to be.

In the following, it will be shown how *In Cold Blood* subtly plays with the notions of objectivity and subjectivity, which are crucial to a work of new journalism. The ultimate aim of the examination of the narrative situation, the style and the figurative language, and the form of *In Cold Blood* will be to trace how Capote uses fictional techniques to (re)construct truth, what effect such techniques have, and, finally, in how far these devices add to (the illusion of) an "immaculately factual" account.

4.1 Gazing, Commenting, Silencing – The Narrative Technique

With regard to the nonfiction novel, Mas'ud Zavarzadeh states that "point of view is basically a variable of the writer's relationship with reality in his narrative" (124). Obviously, in novels that make a truth claim and, thus, explicitly refer to real-life events, the choice of point of view and narrator is crucial in analyzing how real-life matters are being presented. Some types of point of view are more restricted than others, but given that new journalistic works aim at conveying a deeper, more personal truth, restriction is not a drawback. On the contrary, as the analysis of *Armies* shows, the fact that such points of view enable the narrator to give a personal account since they concentrate on the focal character(s) and their perception(s) makes them seem even more appropriate.

As has previously been shown, Wolfe disagrees and considers a third-person point of view common in realist fiction, which enables the narrator to gain access into the mind of every character involved, to be most efficient for an authentic portrait of reality. Since the new journalists wrote about events they experienced themselves, such a point of view naturally suggests a personal union of writer and narrator. This probably explains why scholars in their analyses of works of new journalism often do not distinguish between author and narrator without explaining why. However, many new journalists rejected a third-person point of view since, as Hellmann notes, "the adoption of the technique of omniscient narration commonly found in realistic novels implies a comprehensiveness of knowledge that many writers refused to accept" (15). Given these deliberations, the fact that the narrator of *In Cold Blood* tells the story of the murders in Holcomb in the third person might lead to the following deductions: Firstly, the narrator is identical to Capote; and secondly, he uses the third-person point of view to underline his detailed knowledge about the Clutter case and thus claims omniscience.

While these two assumptions will not be strictly dismissed, the following analysis will display subtleties in the narrative technique which forbid to jump to conclusions and which anticipate a more differentiated analytical outcome. Referring to *In Cold Blood*, Capote once stated that he considered it necessary "that the author should be absent" (qtd. in Nuttall 135). The analysis will gradually unfold to what extent Capote managed to withdraw from making an appearance. As far as the narrative situation is concerned, it will further be of interest in how far point of view and narrative voice support the truth claim Capote makes in writing "A True Account of a Multiple Murder and Its Consequences."

To begin with, it appears to be somewhat problematic to refer to the point of view using the rather traditional term 'omniscient,' as it is often done in critical literature. Hellmann, for example, describes *In Cold Blood* as "a transitional work which is close to conventional journalism in the illusion of objectivity Capote seeks through an impersonal, omniscient point of view" (20). As the literal meaning of the term already indicates, it is the prerogative of an omniscient narrator to have insight into the mind of every character he wishes to talk about. However, the heterodiegetic narrator of *In Cold Blood* rarely reports on the characters' thoughts and, if so, never in an explicit manner, which will be elaborated on below. It is striking that the reader gets to know the characters through the narrator's description and the use of direct and indirect speech but their inner life is rather neglected. Still, other prerogatives an omniscient point of view entails like omnipresence and an overview of the whole past and present plot are made use of. If one stresses these features, Hellmann is generally speaking right to say that an illusion of objectivity is granted through the chosen point of view. The narrator seems reliable and thus objective in that he is capable of changing the setting whenever he wants and does so frequently given the alternating arrangement of scenes. But it is exactly his power to select and arrange scenes as he pleases what is eventually illusory about his seemingly objective account. The fact that the alternating sequence of mostly rather short scenes creates the effect that the novel reads like a documentary might also explain why the narrator widely refuses to gain insight into the characters' minds. By presenting them through descriptions or, most frequently, direct or reported speech, he seems to underline the documentary style of the novel.

Irritated by Capote's choice of point of view, Zavarzadeh remarks that "a contradiction seems to arise between the intention of the nonfiction novel and the point of view adopted in *In Cold Blood*: what is the legitimacy of the use of the seemingly totalizing omniscient point of view in a nontotalizing narrative[11]?" (125). In trying to specify the point of view more closely, he draws the conclusion that "the omniscience which informs a non-fiction novel is based on the writer's thorough research, rather than on his or her imaginative authority" (ibid.). The term he considers suitable to depict the point of view in *In Cold Blood* is thus "'empirical omniscience'" (ibid.). This appears to be a good term to highlight that, unlike writers of realist fiction, new journalists like Capote do not entirely rely on their imagination and the concept of verisimilitude in composing their novels. Moreover, the numerous quotes and excerpts from Capote's interviews with the people involved in the Clutter case as

---

[11] Zavarzadeh uses the phrase "nontotalizing narrative" to point out the contrast to the "classic novel" or "totalizing novel," which imposes order on experience and can, thus, be regarded as a synonym for the realist novel (cf. e.g. Zavarzadeh 6-7).

well as the many documents such as letters, medical articles etc., which he mostly includes in the narrative in full, suggest emphasizing that empirical research builds the foundation for his fictionalized account. However, while Zavarzadeh's term appropriately tries to justify a point of view that claims omniscience, he loses track of the yet prevailing fictionalized nature of the novel. Focusing on Capote's detailed research, Zavarzadeh calls him an "all-knowing author" (125) and claims that he "refrains from any analysis himself; he merely acquires the appropriate documents and inserts them in the narrative" (122). Of course, similar to the selection and arrangement of scenes mentioned above, in choosing from the multitude of documents Capote gathered within more than five years, he had to be highly selective. An analysis had therefore already taken place before Capote began to write *In Cold Blood*. He had to decide which documents to pick – which Zavarzadeh actually already implies by speaking of "appropriate documents" – and where to position them within the narrative.

In his discussion of *In Cold Blood*, which his study *Sentenced to Death: The American Novel and Capital Punishment* positions in the broader context of a negotiation of capital punishment in the United States, David Guest offers a fresh angle on the narrative situation. He pictures the narrator in a panopticon (cf. e.g. 113), which illustrates the power of observation. The narrator of *In Cold Blood* is therefore extraordinarily potent. If one thinks back to the analysis of Mailer's *Armies*, this image is also highly reminiscent of the narrator's idea that the novelist erects a tower for the historian to stand on. From up there the historian is able to look through a telescope and explore every angle of the world no matter how far or near. According to Guest, the narrator of *In Cold Blood* is in the same powerful position, the only difference being that the adoption of Michel Foucault's concept of 'panopticism' entails a focus chiefly narrowed down to the characters of the novel. In his widely noted study *Surveiller et punir: Naissance de la prison* (1975) Foucault uses the term 'panopticon,' which was defined by Jeremy Bentham in 1791 for buildings designed to discipline people, to describe the organization of contemporary western societies. The architectural composition of the panopticon looks like this: An annular building is erected at the periphery and a tower is placed in its center. The tower has huge windows which open onto the inner side of the ring. The building surrounding the tower is divided up into cells each of which is as long as the building is broad. As they have two windows, the light can cross the cells from one end to the other. By the effect of backlighting, the supervisor in the tower is thus able to observe the prisoner, madman, patient, or whoever has been put into the cell. This kind of prison is innovative insofar as the person being observed can never see whether he or she is being looked at since the tower stands out against the light (cf. Foucault 200). Foucault summarizes the effect of this situation as "induc[ing] in the inmate a state of conscious and permanent visibility that assures the automatic functioning of power" (201). The panopticon thus reverses the principle of conventional forms of surveillance like the dungeon but also the principle contemporary prisons are based on in that the captive is at all times observable; "[v]isibility is a trap" (ibid. 200).

Since Guest's idea of the panopticon the narrator of *In Cold Blood* is placed in chiefly serves to contribute to his discussion of the American novel's participation in the reinscription of penal authority, the author mainly focuses on the narrator's observation of the two criminals Dick Hickock and Perry Smith. Considering that the brutal slaying of the Clutter family is the principal theme of the novel and that at least half of the narrative is dedicated to the killers' life stories and their behavior before and after the deed, it is justifiable to claim that the narrator's panoptic gaze favors Dick and Perry. Highlighting the characteristics of the narrator's panoptic vision by comparing it to a first-person point of view, Guest states that "[e]rasing the 'I' from the text may appear to diminish the influence of the author, but instead it allows the substitution of an objective, infallible, panoptic eye for the subjective, fallible, normally-sighted 'I' of the writer" (121). The fact that Guest considers author and first-person narrator of a work to be identical gives reason to assume that, according to him, the same applies for the author of a nonfiction novel and a third-person narrator of the same work. Although Guest does not comment on a possible personal union of author and narrator, it is striking that he grants the supervisor-narrator of *In Cold Blood* infallibility. Connecting this attribute to a 'panoptic narrator' suggests an affirmation of the saying "seeing is believing" – and Capote had been the first to see. However, in that Guest grants the narrator the ability to diagnose (109), to judge from what he sees, he softens the notion of infallibility because a personal diagnosis might also lead in the wrong direction. Moreover, a diagnosis is an interpretation. After the narrator has observed, he must think about what to select and how to present it within the narrative. What Guest is still definitely right about is the observation that "[t]he introduction of the all-seeing narrator recreates the heightened panoptic vision used to scrutinize the prison inmate" (113). Stressing the omnipresent quality of the "all-*seeing*" narrator as opposed to, for example, Zavarzadeh's abovementioned "all-*knowing* author" implies a more skeptical approach, which does not instantly act on the assumption that thorough research equals omniscience.

Judging from these initial deliberations about the narrative situation and its possible interpretations, it is noticeable that *In Cold Blood* both explicitly and implicitly centers on strategies of observation. The numerous quotes as well as the panoptic vision of the narrator leave no doubt about that. One section in which the supervisory gaze of the narrator is particularly obvious is the brief scene in which Hickock and Smith's first night under arrest is described. After having been accused of the murders, the two killers sit in separate cells. They are unable to talk to each other or even see each other, but the narrator is literally in the privileged position of a supervisor in the tower and thus able to observe them (*In Cold Blood* 219-221). While the narrator generally shuns internal analysis, his privileged gaze at times even intrudes into the characters' minds, particularly that of Perry. However, in doing so, he does not simply report on Perry's thoughts through direct or indirect style. Instead, he creates an intricate combination of direct tagged thought, free indirect discourse, and quote. It is thus hard to determine whether the narrator speaks or Perry thinks. This can be illustrated by the following section in which Perry is waiting for Dick to pick him up from the self-service laundry, anxious that Dick has been caught by the police:

> He stood at the kerb retching like 'a drunk with the dry heaves'. Kansas City! Hadn't he known Kansas City was bad luck, and *begged* Dick to keep away? Now, maybe now, Dick was sorry he hadn't listened. And he wondered: But what about me, 'with a dime or two and a bunch of lead slugs in my pocket'? Where could he go? Who would help him? (187)

The narrator could have also gone for interior monologue, but he chose a method that is only seemingly detached. Significantly, that way, his controlling presence extends to Perry's inner life, which clearly shows that he is at no point willing to withdraw completely.

While omnipresence or a supervisory gaze are powerful features, they do not necessarily entail that the narrator is explicit; his power is rather implicitly felt in that the reader is provided with an extensive overview of the story and the characters involved. In contrast, the insertion of quotes, through which the narrative clearly points to an outward reality in which the slaying took place, causes the reader to sense more strongly that there is actually somebody telling and constructing. The narrator thereby prefers three ways to convey that what he says is true. Firstly, he often implies that he has gained information about events through interviews with the characters. In using direct tagged speech, he recalls talks he seems to have had with them. Dick and Perry's dinner with the two hitchhikers they pick up on their way through Texas illustrates that: "After so much activity, even Perry felt starved. *As he later told about it*, 'We carted the old man into the restaurant and propped him up at a table. [...]'" (204, my italics) Secondly, he repeatedly begins a paragraph by introducing a topic and adds the quotation in direct free speech after a certain keyword has been mentioned. An example of this is the section in which Dick is being interrogated by Sheriff Church. The paragraph starts off with the narrator listing Dick's previous jobs and ends with the information that he has once been married to a teenage girl. After Dick's marriage has been mentioned, Dick's verbatim report sets in to give proof and to supply further information: "Before his twenty-first birthday Hickock had worked as a railway trackman, an ambulance driver, a car painter, and a garage mechanic; he'd also married a girl sixteen years old. 'Carol. Her father was a minister. He was dead against me. Said I was a full-time nobody. […]'" (211) Finally, verbatim quotations are often put in brackets to summarize what the narrator also could have told himself. This is, for example, applied during Dick's interrogation and reads like a scientific report in which everything that is written down must be documented: "They talked of everything else: Hickock's religious philosophy ('I know about hell. I been there. Maybe there's a heaven, too. Lots of rich people think so'); his sexual history ('I've always behaved like a one-hundred-per-cent normal') […]" (221).

At some points in the narrative, the narrator's presence is even felt more strongly as he begins to comment. In doing so, he inserts his remarks in brackets. They do not only serve the purpose to provide the reader with extra information but also underline that the narrator is able to explain what he just told. Unlike his strategy to back up his account by tying it to quotes, he now 'forces' the reader to rely solely on his report. For example, when Perry's daily routine of chewing countless aspirins – his only way to subdue the pain he suffers as a result of a motorcycle accident – is being described, he does not miss to demonstrate his knowledge of rather trivial details: "He shook three aspirins out of a bottle, chewed them slowly (for he liked the taste), and then drank water from the basin tap." (52) Such comments serve a function similar to the quotes being inserted in the continuous text. While the quotes are marked as information gained through investigation and authenticate the narrative, the comments in brackets read like paraphrased quotes. Moreover, such 'indirect quotes' are reminiscent of asides in a play inasmuch as after comparatively long sections of telling his story, the narrator seems to feel like he has to turn to the reader and explain why the characters do what they do or something happens the way it does. That way, the narrator adds a more personal tone to the narrative. Since they very often convey extra information which is not crucial for the development of the story, as the example shows, one might wonder why they have been inserted in the first place. It turns out that in this case their primary function is to point out the presence of a narrator. Seymour B. Chatman describes the function of comments as follows: "Commentary, since it is gratuitous, convey the overt narrator's voice more distinctly than any feature short of explicit self-mention." (228)

Apparently, the narrator can hardly become more explicit or, in Chatman's terminology, more "overt" than when he comments. The only way would be to talk about the discourse and to explicitly address and include the reader in the manner of a self-conscious narrator (cf. ibid.) as in *Armies*. While the comments in brackets seem superfluous but constitute a convenient way for the narrator to make himself visible, other phrases indicate that he is also prone to compare and to judge on what he is talking about. Naturally, such rather explicit comments highlight his presence even more. For instance, towards the end of the novel, he does not only insert documents to prove what he says, he even bluntly points out their relevance. Almost as if he wants to reveal his explanation of the murders, he announces that "[i]t is significant that a widely respected veteran in the field of forensic psychiatry, Dr Joseph Satten [...] consulted with Dr Jones" and attaches large excerpts of Dr Satten's article which has the telling title "Murder Without Apparent Motive – A Study in Personality Disorganisation" (290). In depicting Garden City, the community Holcomb is a part of, he further even dismisses a citizen's comment on the alleged equality the townspeople treat each other with saying "but, of course, class distinctions are as clearly observed, and as clearly observable, as in any other human hive" (32). Evidently, he is not willing to rely solely on talk. Instead, he also reserves the right to trust his eyes and to judge from everything that is, as he puts it, "clearly observable." A crucial outcome of his detailed observation is the ability to draw comparisons in order to create a vivid picture in the mind of the reader. This becomes obvious as the narrator makes frequent use of 'as though'-conjunctions. Some of them are used in order to connote the characters in a way that seems to leave no doubt about the narrator's attitude. Describing the atmosphere in Sheriff Dewey's office during the search for the killers, the narrator states: "It was as though, like huntsmen hiding in a forest, they were afraid that any abrupt sound or movement would warn away approaching beasts." (184)

Interestingly enough, in the end, it is a feature that is not as explicit as comparisons, judgments, or announcements which indicates the narrator's power most clearly. Quite cruelly, the narrator initially builds up an atmosphere of a peaceful, pleasant home Mr. Clutter is in charge of, just to end the section by destroying the idyll: "Then, touching the brim of his cap, he headed for home and the day's work, unaware that it would be his last." (12) The same is repeated when he comes to describe Nancy's last evening. She is the prettiest girl and a typical teenager. Her room is painted in blue, pink, and white; she has photos of her boyfriend hanging on the wall; and before going to bed she writes in her diary and sets out her favorite dress to wear the next day. But again, the narrator tears down the scenery foreshadowing "It was the dress in which she was to be buried." (55) It seems as if he has almost prophetic qualities, as if he is not only omnipresent but truly omniscient. He knows about the Clutters' fate and does not only gaze at the killers but also at their victims.

So far, the narrator has given reason to believe that he knows all about the Clutter case. The fact that he 'proves' his assertions in that he includes quotes of people involved seems to authenticate his report. In addition, he appears to be even more reliable since he refuses to naively believe what he is being told. Instead, he tries to draw his own conclusions by gazing and scrutinizing. His eyes, it seems, he can trust completely.

Speaking of a personal union of Capote and narrator, however, remains debatable. Given that Capote laid bare his research methods long before the book was published, one could argue that the numerous quotes make it plain obvious he wrote himself into his work. Yet, if one decides to ignore the context of the novel, this is still left open to interpretation. Interestingly, it can also be argued that Capote makes an appearance as a character since the narrator in passing refers to an anonymous "friend" to whom Perry confides that he does not want to die (312). Knowing that Capote was Perry's only visitor, one can be sure the author refers to himself, but again, Capote's name is not mentioned. It is still not stated explicitly but gets a little more obvious as an ominous "journalist" appears who interviews KBI agent Harold Nye (209) and who is "as equally well acquainted with Smith as he [is] with Hickock" (327). Moreover, Dick gives the decisive hint that this journalist is simultaneously Perry's "friend" saying "'Nobody ever comes to see him except you'" (ibid.). The speculation about a personal union hits its peak if one connects the journalist who appears at the end of the novel to a quote by a citizen at the very beginning of the novel. The anonymous citizen replies to a question which has not even been posed but can be guessed from what the narrator tells about the community. After the narrator has stated that the population of Garden City can be socially ranked, the citizen answers "'No, sir. Nothing like that here'" (32). This of course strongly suggests that the narrator is the one who first interrogated and is now telling his story, and the only journalist with a deeper interest in the Clutter case ever mentioned in the novel therefore identical to the narrator. With regard to the relation between author and text, Thomas Meisenhelder remarks:

[The new journalists] have brought reflexivity to their research. That is, the new journalist often includes himself (or herself) in the story. In doing so, he indicates how he got his information, how he influences his own report. The new journalist forces the reader to become aware of the author's personal presence 'in' the research and how that presence adds to the report. (471)

Considering that even Mailer, who did not claim truth as explicitly as Capote, turned himself into the protagonist of *Armies*, it seems striking that Capote piles hint on hint and talks about his novel wherever he goes but refuses to reveal himself as narrator or character.

Chris Anderson terms Capote's more or less obvious detachment "authorial silence" (48). He is convinced that the narrator is supposed to be identified with Capote and examines what effect Capote's strategy might have. Based on the general observation that "Capote's nonfiction develops from implicitness, restraint, withholding" (56), he argues that "Capote claims a degree of omniscience in *In Cold Blood*" but "for the most part renounces omniscience and maintains authorial silence in the narrative, withdrawing to the point of view of an outside observer" (53). While it remains debatable whether authorial silence or the narrator's more or less explicit comments prevail, there are indeed narrative sections in which the narrator practically vanishes. This can, for example, be accounted for in the second chapter entitled "Persons Unknown." As the first paragraph suggests, its title seems to refer to the murderers, who in the Clutters' death certificates appear as "'a person or persons unknown'" (73). However, Dick and Perry are left unmentioned until late, whereas the main focus of the chapter is put on agent Alvin Dewey and the citizens of Holcomb. They are as unknown to the reader as the killers and must therefore be gazed at as well. Significantly, in this chapter the narrator refrains from commenting almost entirely. Instead, he minimizes his narration to very basic functions; he informs about time and place, describes the different settings, introduces the characters, and gives an account of the incidences taking place. If he did not report on the characters' talk in direct speech, he could even be described as a covert narrator. Thus, the reader is drawn into the action and can participate in Dewey's struggle to make sense of hints and the townspeople's speculation about who killed the Clutters. In this context, Anderson's authorial silence can also be drawn upon to indicate that "throughout his narrative, Capote remains silent about important details" (48). It has been said before that the narrator's comments are explicit but often seem superfluous. The fact that the search for evidence is elaborated on, and that the reader even witnesses Dewey keeping a wrong track while Capote knows better, leads Anderson to introduce silence as a metaphor.

According to him, "silence becomes the central figure for [...] inexplicability" (57), and the murder is therefore "linked to a pervading sense of meaninglessness" (60). The way the narrator introduces the chapter supports Anderson's point. He describes a day as beautiful as the day preceding the murder and contrasts it with the sad task Andy Erhart, a friend of Herb Clutter's, and some others have to perform. They are driving up to River Valley Farm in order to clean the rooms the four family members have been killed in. Significantly, it is said that Andy and the others "drove in silence. One of them later remarked, 'It just shut you up. The strangeness of it. [...]'" (73). According to Anderson, authorial silence apparently links point of view and thematic silence so that Capote's authorial detachment becomes "symbolically important" (67) itself.

In his noted study *The Dismemberment of Orpheus: Toward a Postmodern Literature* (1971) literary critic Ihab Hassan describes silence as a central metaphor in postmodern times and, more specifically, the "metaphor of our [i.e. postmodern] literature" (12). He claims that in times of crises, which can be illustrated by apocalypse, the same image Leslie Fiedler uses to depict the postmodern moment, "[s]ilence implies alienation from reason, society, and history, a reduction of all engagements in the created world of men, perhaps an abrogation of any communal existence" (ibid.). Interestingly, the citizens of Garden City really do begin to lose touch after the Clutter killings. At first, they had been "sufficiently unfearful of each other to seldom trouble to lock their doors," but then came "those sombre explosions that stimulated fires of mistrust in the glare of which many old neighbours viewed each other strangely, and as strangers" (*In Cold Blood* 3). The outcome is, as William Wiegand puts it, "a cacophony of discordant opinion," in which, of all people, postmistress Myrtle Clare, a representative of communication, is "the chief and most articulate spokesman of the new feeling of subversion and isolation" (140). At the very end of the first chapter, she is chosen to convey that the tide has turned in Garden City: "'If it wasn't him, maybe it was you. Or somebody across the street. All the neighbours are rattlesnakes. Varmints looking for a chance to slam the door in your face. It's the same the whole world over. [...]'" (67) It is certainly no coincidence that the next chapter opens with Dewey, the voice of reason, who declares: "I'm going to know what happened in that house: the why and the who." (76) He is the one who is convinced that a rational explanation can finally be revealed repeating: "The link. Got to be one. Got to." (100) But in the end, he is also the one who realizes that "the confessions, though they answered questions of how and why, failed to satisfy his sense of meaningful design" (239). Hassan argues that "[s]ilence fills the extreme states of the mind [...] when ordinary discourse ceases to carry the burden of meaning" (12). When the narrator withdraws, the gap is supposed to be closed by voices of community and justice. However, instead of contributing to an elucidation, these voices have to face that there is apparently no rational explanation for the murders; they are silenced as well and mistrust remains.

4.2 The Facts Do No Longer Speak For Themselves – Style and Figurative Language

Generally speaking, the style of *In Cold Blood* reflects the documentary aspirations of the novel. In the manner of traditional newspaper journalism, the sentence structure is for the most part kept simple and serves the ends of easy readability. Especially in the numerous descriptive sections, the formulations are clear and concise. An example of the rather detached prose style that results from these features is the introduction of the setting, Holcomb, which opens the novel. It is striking that this section is written in present tense, whereas almost the entire story is told in retrospect and thus in past tense. This has the effect that the introductory paragraphs read like a chapter from a geography book. Describing the village and its environment in detail, the narrator locates Holcomb on the reader's mental map of the United States. Phrases like "some seventy miles east of the Colorado border" (1) or parentheses like "[t]he inhabitants of the village, numbering two hundred and seventy" (3) would probably strike one as unusually precise if they did not stem from a nonfiction novel. But it will be shown below that such details serve yet another function than to highlight the factual basis of the novel and the thorough research conducted.

However, ungracious remarks of the narrator and his gloomy word-choice permeate the account-like introduction and destroy the apparent idyll of the dozy village "on the high wheat plains of western Kansas" (1), which might have otherwise easily passed for the setting of *The Wonderful Wizard of Oz*. Right from the start he generates a mystic and forsaken aura that surrounds Holcomb and deprives it of its rural charm. In spite of the "blue skies and desert-clear air," it is situated in "a lonesome area that other Kansans call 'out there'," and the fact that "Holcomb, too, can be seen from great distances" is contrasted by the snide comment, "[n]ot that there is much to see – simply an aimless congregation of buildings" (ibid.). At times, the narrator seems to reinstall the idyll. Without any apparent signs of irony, he, for example, describes Holcomb's environment as follows: "The land is flat, and the views are awesomely extensive; horses, herds of cattle, a white cluster of grain elevators rising as gracefully as Greek temples are visible long before a traveler reaches them" (ibid.). But embedded in the bleakness of his further descriptions, the religious elevation of his simile does come to seem over the top and, finally, ironic.

Interestingly, the occasional silencing of the discourse and the apparent inexplicability of the murders, which are linked by what Anderson calls authorial silence, are also reflected in the representation of the setting. It has been said that Holcomb is depicted as an 'out there'-place hardly anyone had ever heard of until the news of the murders featured in nationwide newspapers after the killings in November 1959. Yet the narrator's description leaves no doubt that it is not only a detached place but also a silent place marked by gradual decay. The streets are "unnamed, unshaded, unpaved" and in the dance hall, the only place that was once filled with music, "the dancing has ceased" and the electric advertisement above the door "has been dark for several years" (ibid.). Even utilized public spaces are already run-down. Mrs. Clare's post office is simply depicted as "falling-apart," and the depot "with its peeling sulphur-coloured paint, is equally melancholy" (2). Besides, River Valley Farm is located in "a mysterious stretch of countryside" (37), and when Sheriff Dewey revisits the Clutter home hoping to detect the decisive hint, he feels the house is unusually silent (149). Once one of the few places in Holcomb that were full of life, it is now "peaceful" like "the great quiet of the prairies" surrounding it (ibid.).

It is, however, important to note that Holcomb is not only depicted as a godforsaken place reverberating with the silencing atrocities that befell the Clutters. The picture of the ghost town sketched at the beginning of the narrative is later supplemented by much more positive descriptions of Holcomb and Garden City in general. The community is also a happy place "where animals and children are safe to run free," and the narrator remarks that "the newcomer to Garden City [...] discovers much to support the defensive boastings of the citizenry" (32). Inserting a quote to support his claim, he shows that for many of its inhabitants, Garden City constitutes a true "'home town'" that conveys a "sense of roots and contentment" (ibid.).

Significantly, like the initial dark portrayal of Holcomb, the more pleasant picture of Garden City is also penned in present tense. Framed by sections describing Dick and Perry's way to Kansas, it comes to read like a snap-shot of the community, an episode in which time stands still while the evil is approaching. The description reads as if no one seems to sense the impending mischief but the position in the narrative underlines that the idyll is threatened. Also, the two documentary sections themselves are contrasted so distinctly that they seem to produce a synthesis; no description is entirely self-contained, the former and the latter Holcomb reverberate in each other. Throughout the novel, the setting is thereby charged with symbolic meaning. The happy days of Garden City are exemplified by a pattern which is as mystic as the unknown Holcomb 'out there:' the garden. Herb Clutter's orchard, probably the most beautiful spot of River Valley Farm, for example, perfectly fits Garden City's pastoral idyll. Evoking thoughts of paradise, Mr. Clutter thinks of this place as "'Eden on earth'" (11). And Sheriff Dewey parallels Herb's love of nature in that he dreams of "his own oasis of oaks and elms" (101). Capote was certainly lucky with names as the real-life setting of his novel is called Garden City and can thus be read as a telling name. According to the sign that welcomes foreigners to Garden City, it is "A Friendly Place" (51). But it is no friendly people who are passing by the sign. Quite ironically, one of them, Perry, does yet carry the same dream inside of him as 'good people' like Herb Clutter or Sheriff Dewey, namely the dream of a garden. Since his traumatic childhood experiences, he has had the recurrent vision that a big yellow bird, a 'sort of parrot' (88), would arrive and "wing[] him away to 'paradise'" (89) whenever somebody hurt him. Moreover, he seems to bear inside him the same religious affiliations that Herb and Dewey's thoughts of beautiful gardens bring to mind. While Herb and Alwin's religiousness is implied in Herb's thoughts of an 'Eden on earth' and Dewey's conviction that "'*Some* day. God willing'" (101) he will have his own garden, Perry is a passionate singer of hymns. Tragically, shortly before the killers are about to arrive in Holcomb, Perry can be heard humming "'I came to the garden alone, while the dew was still on the roses […]'" (48).

Given the local color, the recurrent mythic pattern of the garden, and the second, idealized depiction of the setting, the paradise-like community comes to symbolize the fulfillment of the American Dream. People are religious, friendly, and satisfied with what they have got. Again quite conveniently, the geographical placement of Garden City discloses that it is even situated "in the middle – almost in the exact middle – of the continental United States" (31). Detailed information about the setting shows that the community is located in the center of America, and America's core is about to be attacked by foreign forces. As Zavarzadeh puts it, this means that "[t]he town itself gradually loses its geographical solidity and becomes an emblem of quintessential America, where what happens is less a random murder than a collision between the forces and ideas which have shaped the American Dream" (116), and the narrator himself remarks that "the glamours of the past are today entombed" (31).

Garden City's inhabitants as well as its intruders are described with the same symbolic resonance. Significantly, the narrator relies heavily on the recording of symbolic details, which has been listed before as one of Wolfe's main characteristics of new journalism. By means of this device, the reader is provided with an idea of people's status in life and he is also absorbed into the narrative (Wolfe 47). In order to identify the two opposed forces that clash on the night of 15 November 1959, the narrator puts his focus on diverse details of the Clutters' and the killers' daily routines, which are supposed to allow to draw conclusions about their positions in life. Arguably this works best by comparing the property of the different characters. Already early on in the novel, the juxtaposition of the material possessions is worked out neatly. The reader learns that Mr. Clutter is the second richest man in town (3), and River Valley Farm's interior, though similar to that of other citizens, is "immense modernistic" and representative of the Clutter's wealth (7). In the following section, Perry's "worldly belongings" are being described: "one cardboard suitcase, a guitar, and two big boxes of books and maps and songs, poems and old letters, weighing a quarter of a ton" (12). Clearly, this indicates that the two men come from totally different worlds. The effective use of detail is again demonstrated when Sheriff Dewey revisits the Clutter home. Dewey notices seemingly trivial items that emerge as crucial elements representing the family members they belonged to. On the piano rack stands an open sheet of music, the old folk song "Comin' Thro' the Rye," which Nancy used to play. Mentioning this specific detail causes the reader to imagine Nancy as the girl she was: ambitious, talented, and sharing her father's love of nature (148). Thoughts of her father are evoked next. The "sweat-stained grey Stetson hat" points to Herb's diligent work as a farmer (ibid.). Kenyon's spectacles, however, merely "gleam[] with reflected light" (ibid.). Unlike the sheet music and the hat, they seem to indicate that their owner is never coming back again and reflect the silence of the house. As Anderson suggests, the alleged randomness with which the items have been chosen moreover signals the pointlessness and randomness of the slaying. All in all, it is noticeable that the characters are at first described, which serves the factual claim of the novel, whereas the narrator later minimizes his latent description to a selection of details, which gives *In Cold Blood* the feel of a (realist) novel. Put under closer scrutiny, facts do no longer speak for themselves but carry symbolic meaning. This strategy can be summed up by echoing Anderson's observation that "Capote dramatizes rather than explicates his central themes, relying on symbolism and the implications of concreteness to convey meaning" (49-50).

As much as the community they are living in represents the American Dream, the Clutters finally seem to personify it. Significantly, Holcomb "has an atmosphere that is rather more Far West than Middle West" (1). Evoking further notions of the frontier and the American West, people speak with a "*ranch-hand* nasalness," the men wear "*frontier* trousers," and most houses in Holcomb have front porches (1, my italics). The Clutters, apparently fully assimilated, live American identity and values implied by this highly evocative description. Herb Clutter is a 'self-made man' who works hard and is tightly linked with the rural sphere. He is deeply religious and does not drink. Nancy is the "town darling" (4) and extremely likeable. She is described as "a straight-A student," a "leader," and a "winner" in every way (16). She and her dad form a team as they both take care of the house and people say "'She's got *character*. Gets it from her old man'" (ibid.). Kenyon and Mrs. Clutter, however, are not so lucky in life. Kenyon has barely any friends and Mrs. Clutter suffers from a nervous disorder. But this is not how family members and friends refer to her disease. They prefer calling it "'little spells'" and "'Bonnie's afflictions'" (4). Herb has been a former Eisenhower appointee to the Federal Farm Credit Board and, among other documents, a pompous certificate with the signatures of Eisenhower and Secretary of State John Foster Dulles adorns a wall in his office. Learning that, the Clutters do not only constitute the stereotyped picture of the ideal American family, they become, more precisely, a symbol of the ideal American family during complacent Eisenhower Republicanism and therefore of mid-20th-century America. However, Mrs. Clutter's disease casts a cloud over the apparent idyll in the same way that the depiction of the setting darkens from one moment to the other.

The foreboding of the impending danger is paralleled by the slow approach of the actual danger. Dick and Perry thereby constitute a visible counterpart to the Clutter family and carry equally symbolic weight. As Wiegand correctly observes, "Smith and Hickok [sic!] are identified with the road and the automobile" (139). The stolen black 1949 Chevrolet becomes a leitmotif that signals the urban experience and therefore provides the murderers with a degree of foreignness that enhances their already existent stigma as 'the Other.' As has been mentioned above, the difference between Perry and Mr. Clutter has been established by contrasting their possessions. Now the incompatibility of the killers and their victims is further developed by depicting that they really come from different worlds, the countryside and the city. Quite tellingly, the reader first encounters Perry at a place where he and Dick will from that day forth spend a great part of their time, namely in a quick-stop café. Another considerable part of their time is spent on the road. This is made clear in that the narrator frequently introduces sections about Dick and Perry by referring to the location of the Chevrolet instead of the location of the murderers. The two men are either seen in the car or in cafés and in self-service laundries, and they make their way from Kansas to Texas and Mexico. As they belong nowhere, they are outlaws ready to commit a crime that will seal their lawless status.

Dick and Perry's existence as outlaws is emphasized by the only truly noticeable imagery of the novel. Throughout *In Cold Blood*, notions of hunting charge the already tense atmosphere caused by the tight link between the two main narrative strands, that of the killers and that of the Clutters and Sheriff Dewey respectively. As has been stated in chapter 4.1, the narrator compares Dewey to a hunter while Dick and Perry are Dewey's 'prey,' the "beasts" he is afraid to scare away. In the course of the novel, this image extends constantly. It is not only restricted to Dewey who, at one point, compares his investigation to a "find the hidden animals"-picture (79) but carefully worked out in that it is used to foreshadow the murders and even permeates sections that focus on minor characters. The hunting motif is introduced when five pheasant hunters approach River Valley Farm, which is "not a place that strangers came upon by chance" (11). Sadly, these men are not the only ones who will go hunting on that day. Hunt is moreover connected to the murders in a section that would otherwise serve no visibly important purpose. When Bob Johnson, the life insurance agent who had sold Herb a policy shortly before he died, receives the news of his death, he is just cutting the roast pheasant his wife prepared for lunch. And while Andy Erhart and his friends clean the Clutter home, the narrator quite insensitively remarks that it is "still another fine specimen of pheasant weather" (73).

As much as the Clutters are described as prey to the killers, people regard the killers as bloodthirsty "animals." Those who think of them as "animals" are more or less close to them. Sheriff Dewey's wife Marie is relieved when she learns that footprints are "the one thing those animals left behind" (206), Herb Clutter's brother Arthur is full of hate and wants to see "what kind of animals they are" (271), and in the letter Perry's sister Barbara sends to her brother it says "But if you live your life without feeling and compassion for your fellow-man – you are as an animal" (138). Dick's behavior leaves no doubt that he is the beast people take him for. The reader learns that he likes to run down dogs when he is on the road and he comments the one time he does so in the novel "'Boy! We sure splattered him!'" (108). Perry, on the other hand, does not take pleasure in such random violent acts. Quite contrarily, he even identifies with two grey tomcats which occasionally show up in the narrative and are obviously supposed to symbolize the murderers. The two cats are described as "thin, dirty strays with strange and clever habits" (239). They are hunting for dead birds, which pains Perry to watch because, as he says, "most of my life I've done what they're doing" (256). Homeless and exiled like the killers, they follow Perry as soon as he and Dick arrive in Garden City.

Later on in the narrative, voices are raised that highlight Dick's and Perry's human side. However, such voices are rare. In trial, defense attorney Fleming calls for mercy saying that "'Man is not an animal" and therefore not to be killed (295). And when Dewey witnesses Perry's execution, he notices that "Perry possesse[s] a quality, the aura of an exiled animal, a creature walking wounded" (333). Apparently, the animal image cuts both ways. As soon as the Clutters are dead, the tables turn and the killers are the ones chased, incarcerated, and finally murdered. If this kind of murder is justified remains debatable, but the narrator is definitely keen to negotiate different views on the matter. Even the Clutters do not have an entirely clean slate. There is, for example, also a darker, more despotic side to Herb. He tries to force his daughter to break up with her boyfriend because he has a different religious background (6), and Bonnie remarks "'My husband cares more for those trees than he does for his children'" (11). Besides, shockingly, the shy Kenyon shows a passion for killing as well; only does he kill animals. He is "a good shot" and focuses mainly on coyotes, rabbits, and ducks (37). It can be seen that notions of hunting connect the killers, the victims, and everyone involved. As George R. Creeger puts it, "in denominating the criminal an animal, the community effectively separates him from its own conscious self-image – that of a group of human beings" (110). But the question remains how animalistic the voices are that demand the death of the killers. Echoing Mrs. Clare's reproach that all people are "varmints," the impending mistrust between the townspeople is just another form of exile the community and the state decide to impose on the killers. They are unable to cope with an alien reality, so John J. McAleer ultimately observes correctly that "Capote's topic of prime focus is […] the destructive encroachments of the American Dream" (211).

4.3 The Novel as Prison[12] – Form as Meaning

It has already been touched upon in chapter 4.1 and chapter 4.2 that the characters in *In Cold Blood* are connected in various ways. In terms of the narrative situation, the narrator prefers to gaze at the principal characters but his omnipresent look allows him to put his focus on whoever he wants. The use of the hunting motif and the elaborate animal imagery on the one hand underlines the prevailing notion that the killers are not worth to be treated as human beings, but on the other hand subtly indicates that even their victims are not as innocent as they might seem.

---

[12] This title is borrowed from David Guest's homonymous chapter title in his study *Sentenced to Death: The American Novel and Capital Punishment* (1997).

Another, arguably less eye-catching way to link the characters can be detected with regard to the structure of the narrative. In chapter 4.1 it has been stated that the narrator creates an illusion of objectivity in that he has the ability to switch settings whenever he wants. However, it is the specific arrangement of the scenes, to be elaborated on in the following which already suggests that his way of telling the story pursues a certain goal.

Structurally, the chapters of *In Cold Blood* are composed of self-contained scenes each of which portrays key moments of the lives of the principal characters and sometimes also of the minor characters. The scene-by-scene construction is yet another of Wolfe's main characteristics of new journalism which has been applied in the novel. Comparable to the recording of symbolic detail, this structural device allows to single out pieces of the puzzle which, when pooled together, are supposed to produce a meaningful picture. Moreover, the effect of a mere 'retelling' of the story is avoided. As the new journalist who, like Capote partly does, wants to reconstruct events that took place in the past has to conduct very thorough research before he dares to imagine whole scenes, he has to select carefully what is worth including in his narrative and what is not. Besides, as Nick Nuttall adds, such a strategy "takes the story forward moment by moment, gives it immediacy and, therefore, maximizes the reader involvement" (139).

The first chapter of *In Cold Blood* is told chronologically. After the reader is provided with an explicit sense of the setting and the foreboding of the murders, Mr. Clutter's life story is reduced to a couple of pages before the actual story sets in with the description of the last morning of his life. It is still the morning of 15 November 1959 in the next scene, but this time the focus is on Perry. Interestingly enough, even though linearity prevails in the following scenes, the continuous juxtaposition of two of the three main narrative strands of the novel, the Clutters strand and the Dick and Perry strand, creates a notion of disruption. At first sight, the two parallel strands seem completely disconnected. However, the randomly dropped news of the "four shotgun blasts that, all told, ended six human lives" (3) and the narrator's remark that Herb is unaware of his last day on earth, open a series of allusions to the two foreigners' cruel intentions. The reader, for example, learns about Dick's criminal past, and the shotgun "with a sportsman's scene of pheasants in flight etched along the handle" (20), which he carries with him, establishes an immediate connection with the shotgun blasts that deprive Garden City of its happiness.

Although Dick and Perry's devilish plan is implicitly announced, the tension developed by the cinematic cross-cutting between the scenes does not culminate in the depiction of the killings. Instead, a very short scene that features Dick's joy about the final discovery of the Clutter home and ends with the Chevrolet slowly approaching River Valley Farm is followed by Susan Kidwell's report on the discovery of Nancy's dead body the following morning. But as much as the delay of the description of the murders comes to serve a certain purpose, later to be disclosed, the parallel narratives do more than just generate a tense atmosphere. To some extent, the two strands are constructed as counterpoints. It has been said before that they present a dualism that becomes manifest in the clearly opposed worlds depicted. The symbolic comparison of Herb and Perry's possessions as well as the Chevrolet leitmotif have been perceived as adding to a notion of incompatibility. Extraordinarily coherent connections between the endings and beginnings of most sections, however, argue against the conclusion that the two parties have nothing in common. Perry is, for instance, introduced in that the narrator directly compares him to his first victim: "Like Mr Clutter, the young man breakfasting in a café [...] never drank coffee." (12) In turn, the same scene ends with Dick's arrival, which Perry had been anticipating, whereas the next scene opens with Nancy answering her brother's call. Tragically, Dick, whose pedophile tendencies are gradually revealed in the course of the novel, had originally intended to rape Nancy before killing her. So when Dick announces his arrival by honking at Perry and Nancy calls "'Good grief, Kenyon! I *hear* you" (14), it seems as if she is actually responding to the man who plans on torturing her even more than the other family members. Another link between Mr. Clutter and Perry seems to suggest that the relationship between the two men is more intimate than that between Perry and the other Clutters. Before, their dislike of coffee 'united' them. Now they are connected in that Herb's handshake with the insurance agent is followed by Perry singing a hymn as if to announce and bemoan Herb's death (45). It can also be argued that some of these parallelisms, like the animal imagery, serve to adumbrate that Perry is the more humane one of the duo. Climbing up the stairs to the gallows, Dewey perceives him as a broken man, and while Perry is incarcerated, the two tomcats sit beneath Perry's window, backing him up and ignoring Dick. Dick, in contrast, is mostly depicted as a mindless beast. He repeatedly assures Perry that in murdering the Clutters they will "'blast hair all over them walls'" (20). At a later point, the brutality of this comment is underlined when the narrator connects it to Nancy and Kenyon's more harmless "paint-*splattered* attempt to deprive the basement room of its unremovable dourness" (36, my italics), an attempt to embellish the room Kenyon and his dad are about to be killed in. But the narrator does not clearly pick sides. Later on in the novel, a letter of Bonnie Clutter's brother is published in a regional paper calling on the inhabitants of Garden City to refrain from eye-for-an-eye vengeance since "'[t]he deed is done and taking another life cannot change it'" (103). He argues that "'[t]he doer of this act is going to find it very difficult indeed to live with himself'" (ibid.), but the next section opens with Dick and Perry enjoying a picnic in safety; while the townspeople are reading Mr. Fox's appeal, they are in Mexico.

In the second chapter cross-cutting and parallelism are still applied as technical devices, the only difference being that the Clutter strand is now replaced by the last of the three main strands of the narrative, that of Sheriff Dewey. At this point, the seemingly documentary account loses its linearity as it refrains from abiding by a chronological order. Instead, the movement is not only back and forth between Dewey and the killers but also between the actual story and flash-backs highlighting Perry's past. David Galloway argues that such arrangements "lend narrative drama and thematic richness to the story" (148). Indeed, the narrator almost acts like a movie director. He cuts his narrative, the switching from one scene to another is comparable to pans, and the flash-backs can be described as a way to zoom in on a character as they concentrate on past moments. In this section the narrator clearly settles on Perry in that he introduces three documents into the narrative: an account of Perry's life, Perry's father sends to the prison, a letter from Perry's sister, and a comment of this letter written by Willie-Jay, Perry's former fellow captive. More insightful than these documents, however, is Perry's reaction to them. When he thinks of his father, hate is ultimately the prevailing feeling. Through a long recollection (127-134), the reader learns chilling facts about Perry's childhood. Significantly, this very human account is likely to cause him to be sympathetic to the man who cold-bloodedly killed a family.

At this point, it can be summed up that structural devices of *In Cold Blood* enforce what the narrator's gaze and the figurative language have built up. An examination of the technical devices put under scrutiny has shown that the reader is constantly confronted with notions of intermingling and relating. The narrator's gaze leaves no one out, even though it prefers the principal to the minor characters and (Dick and) Perry in particular. By means of the hunting motif and the elaborate animal imagery, the reader is furthermore made aware that the love of hunting and the act of exiling is not only a perverse prerogative of the killers but permeates even the group of superficially 'good people.' When it comes to the structural division of the novel, the fates of the murderers and the victims are depicted as inextricably bound. David Guests argues that "*In Cold Blood* reproduces the strategies of power associated with modern carceral discourse, 'imprisoning' Smith and Hickock within deterministic narratives" (109). If Dick and Perry are incarcerated in the novel, the reader is their fellow prisoner. From the beginning until the end, the narrative is constructed to absorb him and to cause him to respond emotionally not only to the fate of the Clutters but also to that of their killers. In short, the reader's reception of the novel is being controlled.

The previous deliberations allow drawing conclusions about the 'overall structure' of the novel, referring to paratextual elements like title, subtitle, chapter titles, acknowledgements, and epigraph. The subtitle "A True Account of a Multiple Murder and Its Consequences" has drawn most notice as it reflects and underlines Capote's factuality claim. It suggests reliability and promises answers to a shocking, pointless atrocity. But while details of the killings are exposed, the histories of the killers and the victims are laid bare, and the consequences are described, there is no definite answer as for the question of 'why.' Even more tragically, Dewey, the man who hunted Dick and Perry down, does not feel any satisfaction after he has witnessed the executions. He "had imagined that with the deaths of Smith and Hickock he would experience a sense of climax, release, of design justly completed" (334) but all he can think of is his encounter with Nancy's best friend Susan in the local cemetery almost one year ago. Then, the young woman told him about her life, she mentioned that Nancy's boyfriend Bobby was happily married, and seemed completely content. For Dewey, this is the incident that "had somehow [...] more or less ended the Clutter case" (ibid.). Consequently, the chapter title "Answer" only keeps its promise by answering the question of 'how.' Moreover, Perry's description of the killings is held back until very late, which leaves enough space for the narrator to uncover the human sides of two cold-blooded murderers and the 'cold-blooded' side of ostensibly respectable people. This contributes to the notion that after a thorough reading of the novel, even Capote's acknowledgements, assuring the reader of 'immaculately factuality' granted by the support of representatives of law and order and of the medical sector, as well as a 'mere' translation or insertion of "official records" and "numerous interviews," become less important. Only the striking choice of epigraph reflects an interpretation that is never stated outright but shines through. It is the beginning of François Villon's *Ballade des pendus* and the lines go: *"Frères humains qui après nous vivez / N'ayez les cuers contre nous endurcis / Car, se pitié de nous povres avez / Dieu en aura plus tost de vous mercis."* The speaker, who is about to be hanged, asks his fellow men to pity him and his fellow prisoners just like the narrator is prone to evoke feelings of compassion in the reader. By charging the factual with fictional, symbolic qualities and structuring the narrative in a way that shapes the reader's interpretation, the narrator also manages to point to the complexity of contemporary reality. Nothing is like it seems, as the ambiguousness of the title shows most plainly. The factual echoes the mythic and the present is full of inherent dangers. The impending violent nature of the 1960s is thereby not only represented by the two killers. Capote's (re-)constructed account shows that a more subliminal violence underlies practically everyone.

5 Conclusion

It has been the general aim of this study to arrive at an approximation to the somewhat elusive genre new journalism. The facts that the scholarly exploration of new journalism appears to have had its heyday in the 1970s and 1980s, and that even then only relatively few studies on new journalism were published, caused the decision to set in with a chapter on the backgrounds to and the developments of the genre.

A draft of the numerous tensions the U.S. had to cope with during the 1950s and 1960s provided a useful basis for an attempt to answer the question in how far new journalism was informed by its time. When numerous drawbacks of the respective presidencies of Eisenhower, Kennedy, and Johnson started to show, critical voices were (not only) raised in academic circles. Whereas most writers of fiction decided not to tackle the precarious situation, the new journalists chose subject matters that were closely tied to the intense experiences and the social and political climate of the decades. In doing so, many of them naturally got in touch with and explored the developing youth counter culture, which opposed its authorities in different ways. Similar to the new fabulators' withdrawal into worlds of fable and myth, the hippies took drugs in order to escape from the brutal reality. The beatniks and beats did not confront the values of the previous generation and the decisions of the political leaders as radically as, for example, the various student organizations. Instead, they expressed their opposition through their music and through innovative, provocative writing. Moreover, the cultural concepts of mass culture and postmodernism had an impact on the development of new journalism. While scholars ascribe an increasing sense of alienation and homogenization in society to the dominance of technology and mass phenomena such as mass production and mass media, the conflicting trends in the U.S. provided the basis for a variety of new art forms which were characterized by a fusion of high art and mass culture. It could be argued that it is valid to say that postmodernism entailed a kind of paradigm shift stressing possibility and experiment. Accordingly, the novel was turned into a playful medium that began to cross the border between so-called high and low literature by revisiting, rewriting, and reworking traditional and popular genres. Echoing Fiedler, the gap between artist and audience could finally be closed.

A brief sketch of the development of subjectivity and objectivity, the two doctrines that constitute the most common dichotomy in journalism, was to shed light on the question why a more subjective or objective news coverage may be preferred respectively. Interestingly, this draft has revealed several parallels to crucial tendencies in postmodernism as well as to new journalistic writing. The penny papers' new emphasis on everyay issues, which went along with the democratization during the Jacksonian era, is, for example, comparable to the 'popularization' of the novel in the 1960s. One could argue that the developments in these two different media one day met in the nonfiction novels documenting everyday issues. The sensationalism practiced at the end of the 19th century is moreover reminiscent of the 'spectacular style' that Wolfe attested new journalistic works (, whereas his own style is likely to remain the most 'spectacular' one among all new journalists, considering the colorful, onomatopoeic language and the exploitation of type used in *The Kandy-Kolored Tangerine-Flake Streamline Baby*). After the propaganda following World War I and II had caused journalists to mistrust government and to respond by intensifying subjective or objective coverage respectively, governmental control during the Vietnam War led them to question the more scientific ideal of objectivity and to turn to more subjective reporting.

Consequently, the development of new journalism did not only stem from a mere desire to experiment. It was also shaped by a skeptical attitude towards the possibility of unbiased coverage, by the playful spirit of postmodern art forms, and, as it was able to point out, by the conviction that the decision to write about issues of everyday life in the 1960s entails a reconsideration of common practices. In negotiating scholarly views on the development and the nature of new journalism and the nonfiction novel, the taxonomical uncertainty was striking yet not surprising, given the rather stagnating state of research. However, it was argued for the use of the term new journalism as promoted by Wolfe. If juxtaposed to some of their potential predecessors, the innovativeness of the new journalists can be highlighted. They apply fictional techniques more consciously as it is their aim to provide their accounts with what John Hollowell calls "psychological depth." This means a rejection of reporting in the tradition of a conventional inverted pyramid style or the spirit of mass-media journalism. Instead, they do hold on to a factual basis of their writing but fictionalize their reports in order to live up to an increasingly surreal reality. According to postmodern thinking, which is mainly defined by crossing boundaries, they appear to reconsider the traditional fact/fiction binary and, thus, pursue the general goal faction came to be about, namely the indication of the 'fictionality' of factual discourse. Though a factual subject matter underlies all new journalistic writing, the predominant fictionalization causes that new journalism can pass for a genre of fiction. This, however, does not necessarily mean that it is almost identical to the style of realist writing as a listing of Wolfe's main characteristics of new journalism and the adoption of some of these features in the definition of the nonfiction novel might suggest. Due to the very unique perceptions of reality, the accounts are shaped too individually to be equated with the mode of realist writing.

The analyses of Norman Mailer's *The Armies of the Night* and Truman Capote's *In Cold Blood* served as more practical approaches to the concept of new journalism. It has been the aim to highlight the respective approaches to a representation of reality as they can be expounded by looking into narrative technique, style and figurative language, and form. The examination of these three criteria in *Armies* showed that self-reflexivity plays a major role in the construction of Mailer's account of the peace march. In terms of the narrative situation, the division of the larger first part of the novel, Book One, into the points of view of selective omniscience and editorial omniscience intensifies the facts that the novel is about a personal experience and features a break with mimetic aesthetic which scholars attest postmodern art. As the story is told in the third person and unfolds through Mailer, the reader is granted a seemingly reliable, insightful report. At some points, he is even included in the narrator's reflections on the construction of the narrative. These self-reflexive remarks raise an awareness of the metafictional quality of such parts and, thus, the novel in general. Since the relationship between literature and life is the underlying theme of metafiction, *Armies* can be seen as playing with a confrontation of reality and a 'withdrawal' into the world of fiction. In doing so, the sections in which Mailer is the focal character most clearly reject a comparison with realist fiction because they prefer a factual contract to one promising plausibility. Moreover, according to metafictional theory, a self-conscious narrator can be equated with the real author, so that Mailer's very own 'return of the author' further destroys the illusion of an entirely fictional account.

The emphasis on the status of Mailer's mental state suggested by the choice of fixed internal focalization is, with respect to style and figurative language, enforced by the sentence structure and the word-choice, which both reflect Mailer's sense-making process. The unconventional figures further signal that there is not only one fixed meaning in the world. Without knowledge of Mailer's recurrent imagery, they seem enigmatic. Even Mailer's extensive elaborations on his figures, pursuing the goal to reveal the meaning of the demonstration, are ultimately, in Zavarzadeh's words, "meta-interpretations." Although they clearly criticize the dominance of technology and mass culture, they ultimately strike one as foreign and encoded. Nevertheless, in their extensiveness they can be seen as another form of self-reflexivity. Mailer is the hipster he defined ten years prior to writing *Armies* in that his path to a personal truth is illuminated by his trust in experience and feeling. Meaning cannot be revealed in a rational manner, rather by fictionalizing real-life objects. Mailer's 'factional' metaphors are an important step towards his goal to restore mystery in life and to find back to the most primitive experiences of mankind. According to him, this is the only way to escape from an increasing alienation.

An examination of the interrelation between form and content showed that a lot of structural elements of the novel echo its content. Thus, Mailer's attempt to interpret reality is even expressed in the 'overall structure.' The subtitle indicates most clearly that the concern with possibilities to represent reality is of central importance. Significantly, the narrator eventually even explains the motivation to divide *Armies* into a 'novel' and a 'history' about real life. His self-reflexive contemplations reveal that the fictionalization of history taking place in Book One made it possible to grasp the mysterious character of the incidences in Washington, whereas Book Two was supposed to uncover the background of the event by including articles from a variety of newspapers and by focusing on the initiators of the march instead of Mailer. Although it is revealed in the end that neither Book is purely novelistic or historical, the objectivity claim of Book Two clearly fails. The reality being reported on is too emotionally charged to be represented in an article; the fictionalized 'novel' can best convey the personal experience of a factional reality. Finally, Mailer's skeptical attitude towards journalism, most clearly indicated by his decision to write *Armies* as a kind of alternative to the misleading *Time* article, led him to create a personal account in which he seems to fuse the roles of observer and maker, aiming to experience the event as such and to discover its meaning by examining it from different angles.

Quite contrarily, Capote's "true account" seems strictly impersonal on the surface. However, once the subtleties of the narrative situation are disclosed, the documentary façade of *In Cold Blood* begins to crumble. The third-person point of view suggests reliability but also omniscience, which can be easily used to manipulate the reader. While the narrator's panoptic gaze, enabling him to watch anyone he wants, is representative of the strategies of observation the novel centers on, the latent subjectivity of the account shows in that the narrator becomes more and more explicit. In line with the verbatim dialogue, the numerous quotes included in the narrative are supposed to give it the feel of empirical validity, yet they also imply a personal union of author and narrator, which is already suggested by the statements made in the acknowledgements. Moreover, like Mailer, the real author Capote even seems to appear in his real-life role as a journalist, but he is only mentioned in passing and without exposing his identity. The narrator's presence becomes more explicit as he occasionally starts to comment, compare, and judge in more or less subtle ways. Thus, *In Cold Blood* can also be attested a postmodern break with mimetic aesthetic. The foreshadowing of the murders thereby demonstrates the narrator's knowledge subtly but clearly. In trying to authenticate his account, he heavily relies on the power of sight. He only reduces his presence to nearly that of a covert narrator when his characters are set on the wrong track. Chris Anderson has convincingly argued that this silencing of the discourse, which he calls "authorial silence," connects the narrator's absence as suggested by the point of view with the thematic silencing of the characters. Ihab Hassan's use of silence as the central metaphor of postmodernism enhances this argument. As much as the voices of reason have to face the inexplicability of the killings, silence, for him, stands for a strong sense of alienation, which is reflected by the emerging mistrust between the townspeople.

Like the point of view, the clear and concise style of the novel first seems to add to its documentary feel. However, many descriptions, especially those of the setting and the Clutters, turn out to be symbolically charged. By means of local color and the recording of symbolic detail, Garden City and the murdered family come to represent the American Dream. The killers, on the other hand, are a symbol of urbanity and, thus, stigmatized as 'the Other' by an animal imagery that permeates the novel. Yet this imagery not only underlines the brutality and the exiled status of the intruders. It is also applied to disclose the 'dark side' of the townspeople, who exile themselves by their mistrust. The equally pervading hunting motif even highlights the Clutters' drawbacks, which are otherwise rather mentioned in passing. Interestingly enough, through the reliance on the implications of concrete objects and descriptions, the reader is equally drawn into the action as he is through authorial silence.

The form of the novel, finally, can be regarded as a trap. On the one hand, the characters' fates are sealed in that the community, especially the Clutters, and the murderers are inextricably bound by means of a scene-by-scene construction and a juxtaposition of the main narrative strands. At first sight, this rapid change of scenes seems disrupting and opposing, but allusions and coherent connections suggest that the killings are not avoidable. At the same time, it is striking that parallelisms between Mr. Clutter and Perry as well as flashbacks into Perry's childhood and youth somehow moderate Perry's image as a cold-blooded killer. On the other hand, the reader is trapped in the story as well. The feeling of immediacy brought about by the alternation of scenes causes a desire to get to know the picture that the pieces of the puzzle will create in the end. But his reception is also controlled more distinctly. Paratextual elements like the subtitle or the chapter title "Answer" promise to provide explanations, but in the delayed murder scene only the 'how' is actually answered. Retrospectively, the factuality claim underlined in the acknowledgements thus becomes relatively worthless. Eventually, the epigraph comes to reflect an interpretation which was not bluntly acknowledged but rather shining through.

Ultimately, Mailer's and Capote's novels offer distinctly different forms of new journalism which become manifest in their approaches to a representation of reality. The division of *Armies* into a novelistic and a journalistic account signals a skeptical attitude towards commonsensical ways of understanding. Although, for Mailer, storytelling turns out to be the only suitable way of exploring a fictional reality, he is only able to figure this out by trying – and failing – to write an objective report. In contrast, *In Cold Blood* reflects a faith in traditional modes of sense-making. Its orientation towards the act of observing proves that, according to Capote, conventional ways of understanding still apply. While it is the strategy of *Armies* to conceive the bizarre reality and to openly demonstrate how an interpretation of reality is constructed, *In Cold Blood* presents a ready-made (re-)construction of truth and suggests that reality, though elusive, can be interpreted by means of traditional techniques closely related to realist fiction. In Capote's novel the reader is rather persuaded of the truth being covered; in Mailer's novel he is included in a personal sense-making process. However, no matter how liberal or controlled, both novels constitute valuable contributions to an elucidation of the extreme realities of mid-20th-century America. Mailer, the activist, tackles political drawbacks and arrives at an elaborate analysis of mankind in a technological age, and Capote, the writer, covers an act of violence that could have happened anywhere, anytime and lets it exemplify the downfall of the American Dream in the superficially peaceful Eisenhower era. It is left to examine how other new journalists faced their time, but this should happen as fast as possible because in the recent past a group of writers, the so-called "new new journalists,"[13] set out to take the heritage of Wolfe & Co. to a new level and to show what it means when 'the bastards are making it up' in the 21st century.

---

[13] For an introduction into the new new journalism see Robert S. Boynton's *The New New Journalism: Conversations with America's Best Nonfiction Writers on Their Craft* (2005).

6 Bibliography

Capote, Truman. *In Cold Blood: A True Account of a Multiple Murder and Its Consequences*. London: Penguin Books, 2000.

Mailer, Norman. *The Armies of the Night: History as a Novel, The Novel as History*. London: Weidenfeld & Nicolson, 1968.

Mailer, Norman. *Advertisements for Myself*. New York: Putnam's, 1959.

Critical Literature

Anderson, Chris. *Style as Argument: Contemporary American Nonfiction*. Carbondale: Southern Illinois University Press, 1987.

Baacke, Dieter. *Jugend und Subkultur*. München: Juventa Verlag, 1972.

Begiebing, Robert J.. *Acts of Regeneration: Allegory and Archetype in the Works of Norman Mailer*. Columbia Mo.: University of Missouri Press, 1980.

Blöbaum, Bernd/Neuhaus, Stefan (eds). *Literatur und Journalismus: Theorie, Kontexte, Fallstudien*. Wiesbaden: Westdeutscher Verlag, 2003.

Boccia, Michael. *Form as Content and Rhetoric in the Modern Novel*. New York: Lang, 1989.

Brogan, Hugh. *The Penguin History of the United States of America*. London: Penguin, 1999.

Bruck, Peter. "Berichterstatter oder journalistischer *vates*?: Zur Darstellungssemantik in der amerikanischen Dokumentarprosa." In: Hoffmann, Gerhard (ed.). *Derzeitgenössische amerikanische Roman: Von der Moderne zur Postmoderne: Band 2: Tendenzen und Gruppierungen*. München: Wilhelm Fink Verlag, 1988. 146-164.

Chatman, Seymour Benjamin. *Story and Discourse: Narrative Structure in Fiction and Film*. Ithaca, NY: Cornell University Press, 1986.

Cobley, Paul. *Narrative*. London: Routledge, 2001.

Connolly, Cyril. *Enemies of Promise*. New York: Macmillan, 1948.

Creeger, George R.. "Animals in Exile: Imagery and Theme in Capote's In Cold Blood." In: Weber, Alfred/Haack, Dietmar (eds.). *Amerikanische Literatur im 20. Jahrhundert: American Literature in the 20th Century*. Göttingen: Vandenhoeck & Ruprecht, 1971. 107-126.

Denzin, Norman K.. *Images of Postmodern Society: Social Theory and Contemporary Cinema*. London: Sage, 1991.

Dickstein, Morris. *Leopards in the Temple: The Transformation of American Fiction, 1945-70*. Cambridge Mass: Harvard University Press, 2002.

Eason, David. "New Journalism, Metaphor and Culture." In: *Journal of Popular Culture*,15, 4 (Spring 1982): 142-49.

Emery, Michael/Emery, Edwin. *The Press and America: An Interpretive History of the Mass Media*. Englewood Cliffs, N.J.: Prentice Hall, 1992.

Feldman, Gene/Gartenberg, Max (eds.). *Beat Generation and the Angry Young Men*. Freeport, NY: Books for Libraries Press, 1971.

Fiedler, Leslie. "Cross the Border – Close that Gap: Post-Modernism." In: Cunliffe, Marcus (ed.). *American Literature Since 1900*. London: Sphere Books, 1987. 329-351.

Foster, Richard. "Norman Mailer." In: Wright, George T. (ed.). *Seven American Stylists From Poe to Mailer: An Introduction*. Minneapolis: University of Minnesota Press, 1973. 238-273.

Foucault, Michel. *Discipline and Punish: The Birth of the Prison*. Trans. Sheridan, Alan. London: Penguin Books, 1991.

Frank, Armin Paul. "Literarische Strukturbegriffe und Norman Mailers *The Armies of the Night* [Concepts of Literary Structure and Norman Mailer's *The Armies of the Night*]." In: Brumm, Ursula/Christadler, Martin/Galinsky, Hans/Kessel, Eberhard/Lubbers, Klaus (eds). *Jahrbuch für Amerikastudien: German Yearbook of American Studies*. Band 17. Heidelberg: Carl Winter Universitätsverlag, 1972. 73- 99.

Friedman, Norman. "Point of View in Fiction: The Development of a Critical Concept." In: Stevick, Philip. *The Theory of the Novel*. New York: Free Press, 1967. 108-137.

Galloway, David. "Real Toads in Real Gardens: Reflections on the Art of Non-Fiction Fiction and the Legacy of Truman Capote." In: Waldmeir, Joseph J./Waldmeir, John C. (eds.). *The Critical Response to Truman Capote*. Westport, Conn.: Greenwood Press, 1999. 143-154.

Genette, Gérard. *Narrative Discourse: An Essay in Method*. Ithaca: Cornell Univ. Pr., 1980.

Gilman, Richard. *The Confusion of Realms*. London: Weidenfeld & Nicolson, 1970.

Gitlin, Todd. *The Sixties: Years of Hope, Days of Rage*. New York: Bantham Books, 1987.

Guest, David. *Sentenced to Death: The American Novel and Capital Punishment.* Jackson: University of Mississippi, 1997.

Guttmann, Allen. "Norman Mailer: The Writer as Radical." In: Weber, Alfred/Haack, Dietmar (eds.). *Amerikanische Literatur im 20. Jahrhundert: American Literature in the 20th Century.* Göttingen: Vandenhoeck & Ruprecht, 1971. 92-106.

Haack, Dietmar. "Faction: Tendenzen zu einer kritischen Faktographie in den USA." In: Weber, Alfred/Haack, Dietmar (eds.). *Amerikanische Literatur im 20. Jahrhundert: American Literature in the 20th Century.* Göttingen: Vandenhoeck & Ruprecht, 1971. 127-146.

Hartsock, John C.. *A History of American Literary Journalism: The Emergence of a Modern Narrative Form.* Amherst: Univ. of Massachusetts Press, 2000.

Hassan, Ihab. *The Dismemberment of Orpheus: Toward a Postmodern Literature.* New York: Oxford Univ. Pr., 1971.

Heath, Jim F.. *Decade of Disillusionment: The Kennedy-Johnson Years.* Bloomington: Indiana Univ. Press, 1975.

Hellmann, John. *Fables of Fact: The New Journalism as New Fiction.* Urbana, Ill.: Univ. of Illinois Press, 1981.

Hoffmann, Gerhard, a. "The Sixties and the Advent of Postmodernism." In: Heideking, Jürgen/Helbig, Jörg/Ortlepp, Anke (eds.). *The Sixties Revisited: Culture – Society – Politics.* Heidelberg: Universitätsverlag C. Winter, 2001. 191-235.

Hoffmann, Gerhard, b. "Vorbemerkung." In: Hoffmann, Gerhard (ed.). *Der zeitgenössische amerikanische Roman: Von der Moderne zur Postmoderne: Band 1: Elemente und Perspektiven.* München: Wilhelm Fink Verlag, 1988. IX-XXII.

Hoffmann, Gerhard/Hornung, Alfred/Kunow, Rüdiger. "'Modern', 'Postmodern' und 'Contemporary': Zur Klassifizierung der amerikanischen Erzählliteratur des 20. Jahrhunderts." In: Hoffmann, Gerhard (ed.). *Der zeitgenössische amerikanische Roman: Von der Moderne zur Postmoderne: Band 1: Elemente und Perspektiven.* München: Wilhelm Fink Verlag, 1988. 7-43.

Hollowell, John. *Fact and Fiction: The New Journalism and the Nonfiction Novel.* Chapel Hill, N.C.: Univ. of North Carolina Pr., 1977.

Huber, Werner/Middeke, Martin/Zapf, Hubert (eds.). *Self-Reflexivity in Literature.* Würzburg: Königshausen & Neumann GmbH, 2005.

Huyssen, Andreas. *After the Great Divide: Modernism, Mass Culture, Postmodernism.* Basingstoke, Hampshire: Macmillan, 1988.

Imhof, Rüdiger. *Contemporary Metafiction: A Poetological Study of Metafiction in English Since 1939.* Heidelberg: Winter, 1986.

Jameson, Fredric. "Postmodernism and Consumer Society." In: Lodge, David/Wood, Nigel (eds.). *Modern Criticism and Theory: A Reader.* Harlow: Pearson Longman, 2008.

Johnson, Michael L.. *The New Journalism: The Underground Press, the Artists of Nonfiction and Changes in the Established Media.* Lawrence: The University of Kansas Press, 1971.

Keeble, Richard. *The Newspaper Handbook.* London: Routledge, 1999.

Keeble, Richard/Wheeler, Sharon (eds.). *The Journalistic Imagination: Literary Journalists from Defoe to Capote and Carter.* London: Routledge, 2007.

Kirby, Douglas. "A Counter-Culture Explanation of Student Activism." In: *Social Problems,* Vol. 19, No. 2 (Autumn, 1971): 203-216.

Kutle , Stanley I. (ed.). *Looking for America: The People's History.* New York: W.W. Norton & Co., 1976.

Lee Martin A./Shlain, Bruce. *Acid Dreams: The CIA, LSD, the Sixties rebellion.* New York: Grove Press, 1985.

Mailer, Norman. "The White Negro." In: Feldman, Gene/ Gartenberg, Max (eds.). *Beat Generation and the Angry Young Men.* Freeport, NY: Books for Libraries Press, 1971. 342-363.

McAleer, John J.. "*An American Tragedy* and *In Cold Blood*: Turning Case History Into Art." In: Waldmeir, Joseph J./Waldmeir, John C. (eds.). *The Critical Response to Truman Capote.* Westport, Conn.: Greenwood Press, 1999. 205-219.

McConnell, Frank D.. *Four Postwar American Novelists: Bellow, Mailer, Barth and Pynchon.* Chicago and London: The University of Chicago Press, 1977.

McHale, Brian. *Postmodernist Fiction.* New York and London: Methuen, 1987.

McLaughlin, Thomas. "Figurative Language." In: Lentricchia, Frank/ McLaughlin, Thomas (eds.). *Critical Terms for Literary Study.* Chicago: University of Chicago Press,1995. 80-90.

Meisenhelder, Thomas. "Sociology and New Journalism." In: *Journal of Popular Culture,* 9, 2 (Fall 1977): 467-478.

Meyer, Philip. *The New Precision Journalism.* Bloomington: Indiana University Press,1991.

Mills, Nicolaus (ed.). *The New Journalism: A Historical Anthology*. New York: McGraw-Hill Book Company, 1974.

Mott, Frank Luther. *American Journalism: A History*: 1690-1960. New York: Macmillan, 1962.

Nuttall, Nick. "Cold-blooded journalism: Truman Capote and the nonfiction novel." In: Keeble, Richard/Wheeler, Sharon (eds.). *The Journalistic Imagination: Literary Journalists from Defoe to Capote and Carter*. London: Routledge, 2007. 130-144.

Nünning, Ansgar. "Fictional Metabiographies and Metaautobiographies: Towards a Definition, Typology and Analysis of Self-Reflexive Hybrid Metagenres." In: Huber, Werner/ Middeke, Martin/Zapf, Hubert (eds.). *Self-Reflexivity in Literature*. Würzburg: Königshausen & Neumann GmbH, 2005. 195-209.

Radford, Jean. *Norman Mailer: A Critical Study*. London and Basingstoke: The Macmillan Press LTD, 1975.

Reich, Charles. *Die Welt wird jung: Der gewaltlose Aufstand der neuen Generation*. Wien: Molden, 1971.

Riedel, Wolfgang. "Wohlstand als Krise: Amerika 1950-1980." In: Hoffmann, Gerhard (Ed.). *Der zeitgenössische amerikanische Roman: Von der Moderne zur Postmoderne: Band 2: Tendenzen und Gruppierungen*. München: Wilhelm Fink Verlag, 1988. 31-52.

Roszak, Theodore. *The Making of a Counter Culture: Reflections on the Technocratic Society and Its Youthful Opposition*. Garden City, NY: Doubleday, 1969.

Schudson, Michael, a. *Discovering the News: A Social History of American Newspapers*. New York: Basic Books, 1978.

Schudson, Michael, b. *The Sociology of News*: New York: Norton, 2003.

Talese, Gay. *Fame and Obscurity*. New York: World, 1970.

Waugh, Patricia. *Metafiction: The Theory and Practice of Self-Conscious Fiction*. London and New York: Methuen, 1984.

Wiegand, William. "The 'Non-Fiction' Novel." In: Waldmeir, Joseph J./Waldmeir, John C. (eds.). *The Critical Response to Truman Capote*. Westport, Conn.: Greenwood Press, 1999. 135-141.

Wolfe, Tom. *The new journalism*. London: Picador, 1990.

Wynn, Neil A.. "Die 1960er Jahre." In: Adams, Willi Paul (ed.). *Die Vereinigten Staaten von Amerika*. Frankfurt am Main: Fischer-Taschenbuch-Verlag, 1977.

Zander, Horst. *Fact – Fiction – "Faction": A Study of Black South African Literature in English*. Tübingen: Gunter Narr Verlag, 1999.

Zavarzadeh, Mas'ud. *The Mythopoeic Reality: The Postwar American Nonfiction Novel*. Urbana, Ill.: Univ. of Illinois Press, 1976.

www.ingramcontent.com/pod-product-compliance
Lightning Source LLC
Chambersburg PA
CBHW031222230426
43667CB00009BA/1442